CULTIVATE YOUR LIFE AS A

Mom

MICHELLE BRITNOR

THE GREATEST BLESSING IN LIFE IS BEING A MOTHER

Photography by:

Michelle Britnor, Zoë Britnor

Angelique Bennie, Andrea Wright

With love and thanks, I dedicate this book to the following:

My incredible husband, Travis; without you, our children would not exist nor would I have the incredible title of Mom, I would not be where I am in my journey with Christ, and without your support I would not be where I am today. God has truly blessed me with you and I am so thankful for the Christ centered marriage of love and friendship that we have.

My mom: Wendy. Without you, I would not have had the strong foundation and upbringing that I did, and I wouldn't know what unconditional, sacrificial love is. You have moulded and nurtured me into the woman I am today and not a day goes by where I do not thank God for the mother he chose to bless me with.

My precious children: Zoë and Judah. You are the very reason this book exists. I would not have the experience, the testimonies, the love to share with other moms, had you not been brought into this world. I thank God every day for you two precious angels and I am so proud of the children you are and are becoming. No matter what life may throw at us, I will always love you with all my heart. Never forget that Jesus loves you, as do I.

"May the Lord bless you and keep you; the Lord make His face to shine upon you, and be gracious to you; the Lord lift up His countenance upon you, and give you peace."
Numbers 6:24-26

4

Contents

Acknowledgements

It is a great honour for me to be able to thank those in my life who have made this journey so worthwhile. My mother and best friend, Wendy Wright, thank you for always believing in me no matter how insignificant of an idea I had, thank you for teaching me the importance of family, that money is not the essence of life but that love and the way you treat people is. Thank you for raising me to think with an attitude of love and for not telling me in words but teaching me through example, that a mother is unconditional love, one that puts their children before themselves. The number of times I can recall you saying to me during my life, "No matter what you may do in life, no matter how serious or how much it may hurt you or I, I will always love you and you will always have a place to call home." I pray my children grow to know that same truth that no matter what, I will never love them any less, they will always be my babies! Thank you for teaching me that I can do anything I put my mind to, you have proven right over and over again and I love you more than I often tell you. My dear husband Travis, thank you for being so supportive during this book writing adventure, for reading my book even though you are a man and cannot relate, for listening to me and doing so much of what I usually do whilst I dedicated hours to writing. Thank you for being my teacher, I am truly blessed to have a husband that is so committed to God, an all or nothing kind of man that has put God in his all category and devotes his life to honouring and serving God. Thank you for teaching me as you learn and being patient, learning that although it is difficult and frustrating, it is also possible, to have a conversation with constant interruptions of "stop that, what is going on, in the bath!" I love you, and I thank God for the man He chose for my journey through life! Thank you to my mother and father in law, Antoinette and Leon, for the incredible son they raised and for the blessing they have been throughout our journey. No words can express how thankful I am to have you both in my life. A big thank you to my aunt, Yvonne Dunnington, Ludene Lefevre and Elmarie Kinsey-Ahlers, for reading through my book and giving me the encouragement I needed. Elmarie, thank you for checking it over with a teachers eye in mind and Ludene your friendship and your support through this time has been such a blessing, I thank God for putting you in my life, you are a true treasure. I thank every person who I have had the honour of meeting in life, not only those who have been a positive influence but also those who have hurt me, I have seen how not to treat people and have grown to become a stronger, independent woman who cares more for those around her than she does for herself. My so many friends, there are too many to mention everyone but there are many I have had since childhood and one even since birth, thank you all for the way each of you have touched my life in a different way. Each of you got me through a different place in my life and brought me out to where I am today. I do not want to name anyone for fear of missing someone but know that you are all loved and I am so very thankful to have each and every one of you in my life, even those who I may not speak to for months but the bond is never broken. And last but not least, I thank God for being my everything, for being the one constant in my life, that in an ever changing world filled with ever changing people, ,my Daddy God remains the same, His love and His promises never change and never fail me. I only pray that perhaps this book touches, even a portion of the ladies who read it and perhaps lead them to have a deeper relationship and understanding of the Father God I know and love. I pray that whatever you are going through, you would know you are not alone, whether you feel like a terrible mother for something that no other mother seems to go through, know that not everyone shows what happens inside, most only share the good things but you are not alone. If you are in a place where you feel alone or need prayer I would be so

happy to chat to you, please contact me and I would love
to share your journey with you!

Cultivate your life as a MOM

Introduction

Being a mom is hard work... if you're doing it yourself. If you're not fobbing your kids off on friends or family at every opportunity you get so that you can live YOUR life. Ask yourself first, why did you have children? Did you have children because you wanted to raise them, teach them and love them? Or did you simply follow the cultural expectations with the worldly thinking of, "All my friends are having babies, I'd better not miss the bus."

Being a mom is not something to be taken lightly. It is a gift that God has chosen to give to *you*. If you are a single mother, having children and having to work should not be a burden. Hard work yes, exhausting yes and at times you may want to give up, but this should never reflect on your children. They cannot help whatever your circumstances are, it is not their fault that you have to raise them by yourself and have to work instead of having the support of a husband; they are only children. We are given the choice of free will in life. We can choose to follow the pleasures of the world; or live a life of righteousness through Jesus Christ. You brought your children into the world and when you change your perspective to realizing that even though you are doing it as a single mother, God has given you that child to make a difference. To be part of a greater generation, and when you realize that this child doesn't understand your situation and that all you can do is love them and that they are not a burden to you, then you will be able to raise a "New" Generation. A Christ filled generation...

Mom is a title far greater than any title the world could give you. Teacher, Doctor, Accountant, Judge, Lawyer, these are all fantastic achievements however no title or achievement compares to that of being a Mom. You are chosen to raise your children to be God pleasing, upstanding citizens in a generation where the world is a crazy place obscured with sadistic, evil connotations to just about everything. Children's cartoons, games, music, majority of these things are in most part, not right for our children. Look at how the age restriction has changed in movies from when you were a child to now, look at how many children under the age of 5 can use that four letter disgusting word that doesn't belong in that innocent mouth. So many things of today are wrong with the world yet how many parents teach their children otherwise? How many stand up for what is right and say NO! You will not watch that show because it teaches you to be aggressive and it allows evil into your life and into our home? Or how many think, it's just a cartoon, it's not scary? Who's level is it not scary on? Yours or your 3 year old child who is watching a creature getting its ears cut off? Your children have an incredible future destined and with God's help, God's direction and God's word, you will equip them with the tools to lead the life they are called to, a life with purpose.

I am a wife, a full time mother of 2 beautifully incredible little souls, a cook, a maid, a doctor, a playmate, a friend, a daughter, a photographer and many other things. Being a mom is no easy task; however it is the most rewarding opportunity God could have ever blessed me with. I would never trade it, not my husband, my children, my simple yet extremely busy lifestyle, my financial situation, none of it. Nothing about this life is easy, if it was we wouldn't need a savior, we wouldn't need a Father to cry out to when we couldn't do things in our own strength. If life was to be easy, there would be no division of good vs bad, there would be no hard decisions to make and there would be no hope for our entire world's population. Sin is what makes this life difficult, it is not the struggle to do good but the struggle to not sin. It is a struggle that everyone faces daily; yet some people ignore their sin because life is easier without having to choose to avoid it. Although my life is not always easy and I sometimes struggle to deny my flesh of the sinful pleasures of the earth, when I hear that Jane Doe down the street met Joe Bloggs for a cup of tea while her husband was out of town, I have to remind myself that I am in Christ and Christ would not condone listening to or sharing that information that had nothing to do with me, so although it is not an easy walk through life, I would change NOTHING! Why? Because I am exactly where God wants me to be! Are you?

Do the things that bring you joy!

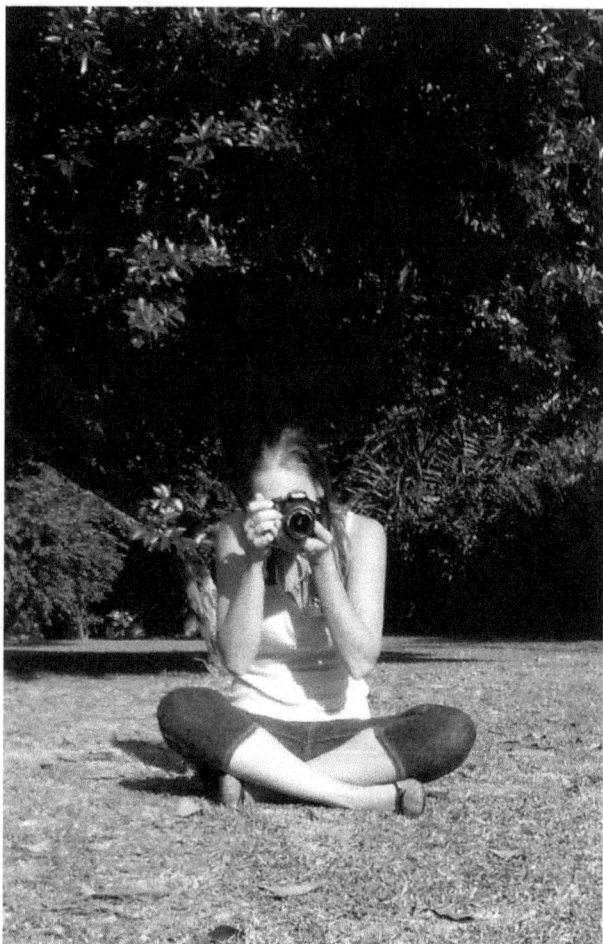

CHAPTER 1

Cultivate your own life

Are you at a place in your life where you feel if God was walking beside you, He would be happy? God walks beside you daily, he sees everything, hears everything and knows everything before it is to happen. Do you think God is pleased with you and that you would join Him in heaven when He calls us home? What we don't realize is that each and every one of us are born sinners; big thanks to our descendants Adam and Eve for that! The Bible says we need to work out our own salvation with fear and trembling. (Phil 2:12) This action is not a once off done deal, it is a way of life, a choice to live a life that pleases God. A daily cloak of righteousness we choose to wear that when we walk down the streets people feel the presence of God coming with us before they see us. For God said in Genesis 1:26, "Let us make man in our image, after our likeness..." If we are made in the image of God then why are we striving to be like other sinners around us? If God is our all powerful Creator who sent His son to die that we may live, then why do we live to impress man rather than live to impress and serve God? So many people, even those who believe they are Christians and they are saved, have not been taught what it truly means to be a child of God, a follower of Christ, to be In Christ. Our joy should come from making God happy, not worrying what others around us think or who we may offend with our love for Jesus. Matt 10:33 "But whoever denies me here on earth, I will also deny before my Father in heaven."

Being a true Christian, is simply to realize that you are a sinner and to put on that cloak of righteousness, breathe in Jesus Christ and never let out that breath. To hold onto Jesus even when you feel like you have no strength, to never let go. 2 Corinth 5:17 "Therefore if anyone is in Christ, the new creation has come: The old has gone, the new is here!

This doesn't mean that, ok sure, I accept that Jesus is my Savior and He came to die for my sins that I can be saved, *however,* it is too difficult to devote my life to sharing God's word, I would rather focus on becoming successful and having a big house and owning boats and Ferrari's etc. If that's your mentality then I ask you this, do you think you are truly saved? When you are In Christ, living a life that pleases God is not work, its not difficult, it comes naturally. Yes there are times where we may have two choices and our sinful nature may get the better of us, but we should strive to deny our sinful side and turn back to righteousness. If you want to live a life of purpose, joy, love and meaning, you need to live as Jesus did. It may not always be easy, but we serve a loving God who knows our hearts, He sees our efforts and knows our intentions when we mess up. When we repent, He is quick to forgive us because we are His children. Jesus came to save the sinners, if we are all sinners as the Bible says, then Jesus came for each and every one of us. No one sin is greater than the other, God despises all sin, but Jesus came to stand in your place and say, I have paid the price for this soul. She is Mine! I have called her by name. Something rather incredible was pointed out to me last night. Look at the veins on the palm of your hand, both hands, look carefully and on each hand you should be able to identify a letter "M" with the lines. How incredible that God marked each and every one of us with the M, "I have called them by name and they are Mine!" Live your life as a testimony that you are His!

FULFILL YOUR PURPOSE

God created you for a purpose. So many people get their purpose and their function confused... ALL the time, up until a few years back I could not answer the question, "What is your purpose?"

I will start with your function as it is shorter and less detailed. Your function in life is where you need to be to sustain normal living, for some their function is doctor, for some a caregiver, for some it is to do volunteer work with no pay. Not everyone's function is the same. My primary function is a wife, my secondary function is a mom, then housewife, then photographer and author. We have several functions in life, but our function should never take priority over our purpose. Our function should be used to fulfill our purpose. We should be the window of hope and love that people get to see or meet on a daily basis. How many of us occasionally go to town in a really bad mood, everything is going wrong, the kids don't want to get into the car, then you finally get them buckled in and on the way you are sitting behind a trail of non-moving traffic, then eventually you get to the mall and your kids don't want to get out of the car. Finally you get them out of the car and your heart skips a beat as one of them tries to run away from you as you scream after them, COME BACK HERE! I'm going to count! You get to town and you haven't even started shopping yet but already you wish you were done and at home. You drag your nagging, moaning, hungry and thirsty kids, who ate and drank in the car 15 minutes ago, through the shop, you get to the till and feel like you've just been in a boxing ring and the teller looks at you like you've lost the fight. What kind of person would you really appreciate to see sitting behind that till? Someone who doesn't greet or smile, throws your shopping to the other end of the counter, gives you a filthy look as you pay and sends you on your way with the incorrect change, or a happy, smiling person who greets you with enthusiasm and asks you if you are alright, packages your shopping with care and helps you along in a gentle manner, even maybe speaks sweetly to your children and noticing how flustered you are, suggests they just sit nicely and listen to you. Which type of person would make you happier? Whatever workplace you are in, you impact someone, whilst carrying out your function, the way you live, the attitude you have and the love, joy and friendliness you show, should fulfill your purpose. People should want to come back and see you again because they love being around you because you portray a good God who is nothing but love. Colossians 3:12 "Therefore as God's chosen people, holy and dearly loved, clothe yourselves with compassion, kindness, humility, gentleness and patience." Colossians 4:6 "Let your conversation be always full of grace, seasoned with salt, so that you may know how to answer everyone."

What is your purpose? Some folks might say, "I know my purpose, God wants to see me blessed, with a big house, a fancy car, my own business which puts millions in my pocket so that I never have to go without. God wants to see me rich; my purpose is to be rich!" Anyone feel like that? All of those things sound lovely right but you're wrong.

Is being a mom scary? Is it difficult? Of course it is. In this same way, being a true Christian, a Christ follower, is not easy, it is difficult. No one wants to hear that. We all want to hear how to live that easy life full of pleasure, lots of money and everything that is better than what someone else has. Your purpose is not to be rich, who are you living for; God or man? Why do you want to be rich? So that you can show off and be boastful in front of man? Would being rich glorify God and make Him happy and further the kingdom of heaven?

Your purpose, your primary purpose on this earth, is to praise God, to bring Him glory, to make Him happy. No it's not easy but Jesus said in Luke that we should count the cost of following Him. You are either in it 100% or not at all. Why would we want to do anything other than live our life for our Creator? Well, many people miss the mark on this one simple thing. When you look at the world around you, don't you wonder what it will be like when our generation falls away and our children's generation is to carry on? What education will they have? How safe will they be? What kind of jobs will they get? I'm a mom, I get it, I think about these things too. Could you imagine looking at this world, the sin of every person in the world and knowing the only way to fix it would be to sacrifice your only child?

As a mom we do all we can to protect our children. Some of us I'm sure would wrap them in bubble wrap if we could, so I'm sure no one could even imagine sending your only child to death to save the rest of the world. God did this! God sent His ONLY Son, He sent Him knowing that He would me mocked, ridiculed, beaten, spat on, tortured and hung on a cross with nails pierced through his hands and feet whilst blood spewed from the gaping wound in His side. God sent His ultimate sacrifice for YOU to be saved because He knew that you couldn't do it alone. Is that not reason enough to give your entire life to God, to choose to do what He wants instead of what you want?

This was Jesus' purpose. His purpose was to die on this earth so that we can spend eternity in heaven with our Father. His purpose was being obedient to God even though it meant he had to perish on earth. His purpose brought praise, honour and glory to the name of God because He walked with love, He despised sin, He offended people because of His love for God but He fulfilled His purpose, regardless.

Romans 3:23-24 for all have sinned and fall short of the glory of God, and are justified freely by His grace through the redemption that came by Jesus Christ.

We are saved by grace, yes. However, does that give us a ticket to lead an unholy, worldly life that makes us happy? Or should we live a life that is pleasing to God?

Carrying on from Romans 3:24, Romans 3:25-31 "God presented Him as a sacrifice of atonement, through faith in His blood. He did this to demonstrate his justice, because in his forbearance he had left the sins committed beforehand unpunished - he did it to demonstrate his justice at the present time, so as to be just and the one who justifies those who have faith in Jesus. Where, then, is boasting? It is excluded. On what principle? On that of observing the law? No, but on that of faith. For we maintain that a man is justified by faith apart from observing the law. Is God the God of Jews only? Is he not the God of Gentiles too? Yes, of Gentiles too, since there is only one God who will justify the circumcised by faith and the uncircumcised through that same faith." *Here's the most important part of this whole passage...* verse31: "Do we then, nullify the law by this faith? Not at all! Rather, we uphold the law!"

So, our purpose being to praise, glorify and uphold the law. Let me first say, upholding the law without faith does not buy you your spot in heaven. James 2:26 "For just as the body is dead without breath, so also faith is dead without good works."

Your works alone cannot buy you eternal life just the same as believing in Jesus without bearing any good fruit cannot buy you eternal life. Even Satan believes in God yet he is not saved because he does not produce good works. God knew we would not be able to fulfill the requirements of the law. This was His purpose in sending Jesus. Matthew 5:17 "Do not think that I have come to abolish the Law or the Prophets; I have not come to abolish them but to fulfill them." We need to keep to the commandments because Jesus said, if you love me you will keep my commands. And Matthew 5:19-20 carries on to say, "Anyone who breaks one of the least of these commandments and teaches others to do the same will be called least in the kingdom of heaven, but whoever practices and teaches these commands will be called great in the kingdom of heaven. For I tell you that unless your righteousness surpasses that of the Pharisees and the teachers of the law, you will certainly not enter the kingdom of heaven."

Surrendering your life to God is choosing to be in Christ. To be in Christ is to walk as Christ walked. When you truly give your life to God upholding the law is not a requirement because we are saved by grace, however every day you should strive to carry them out because of your obedience to God and because you love him. You sacrifice your wants and desires to fulfill the purpose God has requested of you; this suffering does not mean you live a miserable life. The life God wants for you is more incredible than you could ever create without Him. What I have today, I would never have accomplished without God. It cannot be seen in my bank balance or in the car I drive because they are not materialistic blessings; they are soul jolting, heart pleasing, life breathed blessings. Jesus told the rich man to go and sell all he owned and then he could return and follow Him. Following Jesus should be an honour, not a burden. He gave His life for you, surely you can live your life for him!

When your children listen to you, do you not feel as though they love you enough to listen? In this same way when we are obedient and we listen to God, we show how much we love Him, that we appreciate Him and we are willing to do whatever it takes to show him how thankful we are for the gift that no man could give us today; the gift of His only Son and the gift of eternal life.

How do we honour God? We keep His commands. We teach others to keep His commands. The two greatest commands given are simple: Love the Lord your God with all your heart and second which is as important as the first, is love your neighbor as yourself. With these two commands we can live a Christ filled life. All of the commandments come down to just those two. Those two alone can at times be challenging.

When the old lady cuts you off in traffic when you're late to take your child to school, how do you react? Do you tell her off as you throw your fist up in anger even though she cannot hear you, yet your child in the backseat hears and sees it all. Or do you pray for her and thank God for sending this dear old lady to slow you down a bit whilst you catch a glimpse of your little one's smile in the rearview mirror. Sounds ridiculous right, everyone gets angry. Yes sure, we are human and we have emotions but we need to train our emotions. When you catch yourself with your hands in the air saying, "What are you doing, don't you know I'm late?" remember that God too, sees all. When the Holy Spirit convicts you, repent and pray for both yourself to calm down and for the woman you're waving your hands at.

When we see or hear something of the world and not of God we should turn from it, rebuke it and turn our focus to our Father. We are all sinners as the Bible says in 1 John, "If we claim to be without sin, we deceive ourselves and the truth is not in us." But when we do sin, which is inevitable, we need to repent. What does it mean to repent? We cry out to God, we beg him for His forgiveness and we apologise for what we have done.

That's where most people end their repentance; they miss the last vital step. Turn from your sin and do all you can to never do it again!

Praise God, thank Him daily, devote a portion of your day to spend time ALONE with Him. Pray, read your Bible, download biblical teachings to listen to, listen to some of your favourite praise and worship songs. One of the commands is keep the Sabbath holy. The Sabbath being the day of praise, the day of rest, the day you give to God. Give every day to God; make every day the Sabbath. Praise Him throughout the day. When something goes right in your life, do you celebrate the victory with three bottles of wine, a huge party, a big display of how fantastic you are that you did it? Or do you celebrate with thanks to God, thanking Him for helping you to make it out of the place you were in, for making you victorious? Is it about you or about God?

When things are really bad in your life, you lose a loved one, or even something as simple as a blown tyre on your car. Do you find yourself thinking, God why me? Where am I going to get the money for this? Why did God let this happen? God knows your situation; God places things in our lives for a reason. I am a firm believer in "everything happens for a reason." You may have missed a three car pile-up that could've taken place had your wheel not blown, you may meet someone who comes to tow you away that really needs to know Jesus and God has placed you there to shine, to plant the seed that is needed, a loved one may pass on and you're hating on God for taking this person away. That person's death may bring someone to Jesus, and although its hard in the flesh to understand, isn't the fact that your loved one is safe at the right hand of God a comfort and then even more so, that in their death they have eternally saved another soul that was otherwise damned to the pits of hell? They did not die in vain; they died for their "purpose." Their purpose brought glory to God even in their final days. There are things in life that happen that are beyond our control, God doesn't bring bad things upon us. One of the worst sayings I so often hear is, "Why does God let bad things happen to good people." I want to rip my hair out when I hear this, yet I used to be one of the people saying it. Satan is the one who comes to steal and destroy, when he attacks us in life, God through His Holy Spirit sends us ways of coming out on top of whatever we are going through. When we aren't listening to the Holy Spirit, when we think we know best, God can't help us. When we are in a bad situation there are two doors, God says choose this door, it may not be easy but you will make it in the end. Most of the time people decide to rather go through the other door because they know better; they can do it without anyone's help. That is when bad things happen to good people. It's when good people listen but don't hear, or they do but they ignore that still quiet voice. God gives us the tools but we need to pick them up and use them.

Another important part of carrying out our purpose is to have faith. Faith is more than just believing in God, in Jesus and the Holy Spirit. Faith is a lifestyle. Sounds easy however faith is something we need to work on daily. Too often we try to do things in our own strength instead of giving it to God. When you look at your budget a few days before your salary comes in, or if you're like I used to be, and you try to recalculate your budget several times in the month as though something is going to change, you look at it and you're short for this and short for that and you think, how will I ever do this? Your question is the problem in your budget.

We have all had debt. Most of it unnecessary debt, a fancy new car for instance is an unnecessary debt, buy the car you can afford that goes forwards and backwards. What is your reason for buying the car? Is it to show it off to the world, or to get from A to B? Clothing accounts are unnecessary debt. There are people in the world who wear the same shirt 7 days a week, they bathe in rivers, rinse their shirts in the river and put them dripping wet, back on their bodies to hopefully dry in the sun. Most of us have closets FULL of clothes, deciding what to wear is a problem because there are too many choices right? Why do you then need more? Cellphone accounts! Does your cellphone work? Then leave that new pretty one in the shop if it's not seriously within your budget. If you need a new phone, it doesn't have to be the latest most expensive one, who are you going to impress, you'll get a few reactions of, "ah wow", and within a week your expensive bragging device will no longer be the latest coolest trend but you'll still be paying the debt off over the next two years! TWO YEARS!!!!

So getting back on topic, write up your budget, write the amount your debts are and put all your efforts into paying your debt. The burden of debt is not worth it. Once you have your budget on paper instead of asking that dreaded question, "How am I going to do this", turn your focus to your purpose. FAITH! Thank you, God, that you know my needs, you are Jehovah Jireh, my provider and this budget, my finances are in Your hands. I cannot do this but You can. And watch when month end rolls around how God comes through, be dedicated, take away your luxuries to pay your debt. I'm sure you hate it when people owe you money. It's your money; they should have paid you back! It's the same with accounts. Your money is not your money as long as you have debt.

When we first got married, both my husband and I were working full time, we were swamped with debt and we weren't able to even pay some of our accounts. We got to a point in the month where we were running out of groceries and we had no money. Now some people view having "no money" as, well we only have enough for the rest of the month and our savings is for school for the kids etc. When I say we had no money I mean, no savings, our bank balance was zero and our pockets were empty. Even the tips from the laundry box (my husbands pocket change) was empty. We asked God, what are we going to do? We then turned our wrongful thinking to focus on God, only He could get us out of this situation. On arriving home from work that day, we went inside to unwind. Not 10 minutes later there was a car hooting in the driveway. When we went out there was no one, no car, no person, no note but three bags of shopping. To this day, 6 years later, we still have no idea who it was and nor do we question. We purely thank God for whoever it was, that they were obedient to God when He commanded them to do it. God can do the impossible, He can make your impossible budget completely possible if you only listen to Him and follow His will for your life. He puts people in our lives, speed bumps to prevent us from going in the wrong direction and places us where we need to be. It is our faith that allows us the opportunity to see the fruits of His work. Be the woman Christ intended you to be, praise Him, Glorify His name and have faith, because Phil 4:13 says "I can do all things through Christ who strengthens me." This is my ultimate, favourite scripture in the Bible; it applies to absolutely everything in life. To be the best possible you, you need God first in your life. The rest should follow.

Fulfill your purpose, let everything you do be a reflection of God's goodness, do not be ashamed of your Father, speak His word, praise and glorify his name, devote your life and your time to God and teach others of His word. Consider the salvation of those around you and tell them of the good news that they too can be saved. Jesus shouldn't only be the words out of your mouth, He should be your lifestyle, you should ooze the love of Christ so that when people look at you, they can see Christ in you without you having to mention His name. This is your purpose, this is the very reason you were created, the only one who will be judged on your life is you, no one can fulfill your purpose for you. Cultivate your life the way God intended it to be. Fulfill your purpose!

GET SOME REST

Mark 6:31 – And He said to them, "Come away by yourselves to a desolate place and rest a while."

As a woman, a wife, a mom, we get stressed. Super stressed, we stress about things men don't stress about and then stress even more because they aren't stressing about it. We stress about our children, our husbands, our friends and family, our finances, the latest strain of flu going around that could infect our children, the state of the house because our toddlers are too small to tidy up their mess and we are the maid, we stress about EVERYTHING! It's easier said than done but we need to take a break from that. Our bodies need rest and time out. So do our minds, how often do you feel, "For my sanity I need silence for a moment, just a moment." But you have a toddler who follows you to the toilet, a husband who needs you to help him find a pair of socks, the laundry needs doing, the dishes are piled to the roof because your kids keep bringing new cups and plates for snacks and juice. I often think, can everyone just calm down and give me 5 seconds to even fill my lungs with air and let out a breath. God created us to be able to do all these things and still function like a human being even though we sometimes feel like robots. God intended for us to rest though, that is why the Sabbath is so important, but as I said previously, make every day the Sabbath. Along with praising God daily, try to rest daily. Even if it's half an hour when your husband is home, leave the kids in the lounge, he's probably watching TV anyway, he'll hear if one chokes, (You're thinking yeah right, when he watches TV he doesn't even hear me when I speak) but I can promise you when you put your child in your husband's care and he can see that you trust him with your children, he will look after them. He also loves his children and wants no harm to come to them. I am very much a control freak, no one can look after my children the way I do, right? Anyone agree? In a sense yes you are right, no one loves your children the way you do but your husband has the same amount of love for your children as you do. He loves them as much as you do he just has a different bond with them and he probably doesn't get the chance to be as responsible for them as he would like, because if you're anything like me it has to be done my way or it's wrong, this is something I struggle with daily but with God's help, I am learning to loosen the reins, I have come to realize that it is not my way, it is God's way.

Getting back to my point which I so easily get distracted from (I'm sure our brains don't function quite the same after having children), you need time to rest, leave the kids with your hubby, tell him you are MIA for half an hour and be by yourself. Read a book, have a bubble bath, or do both at once. I find my head is constantly filled with noise, when I wake up in the night to use the toilet, I'm singing in my mind the theme song of one of the latest cartoons. There's never just silence in my head and it's tiring. My favourite time out is lying in the bath with my ears under the water. All I can hear is the gurgle of the pipes, I can't hear the TV, kids crying because my 2 year old wants my 4 year old's toy and they're tired because it's been a long day and its nearly bed time. I can't hear if I'm getting messages on my phone or anything that's going on in the big wide world. I just close my eyes and for once, it's silent. I find some days if I've had a real difficult day and I climb into the bath, I'm uptight, possibly frustrated and have been moaning at everyone because of the day I've had that feels like it's just never going to end. But the minute I climb out of my resting bath, I have a renewed peace of mind, once dressed I find instead of being angry or frustrated I am thanking God that I have been blessed with such an incredible family and asking God to forgive me for taking my daily frustrations out on the ones I love. Although they sometimes frustrate me because they don't listen because they are so young and because everyone needs mom, God has blessed me with children that some people never get the opportunity to have. I have been blessed with an incredible, God-centered, marriage; where there are others fighting to get away from abusive husbands. My marriage is my number one blessing, without my husband I wouldn't have my two beautiful children and I probably wouldn't be where I am today in my journey with God.

As a stay at home Mom, I am with my children all day every day. I home school my 5 year old as well, so I can tell you, I honestly understand how you sometimes feel like just running away, just for no one to need you for at least 5 minutes, but you have the most precious gift life has to offer. My children eat ALL day, I feel like I spend the majority of my day making food and juice and think how nice it would be if they could get it themselves; and then I find myself thinking about how quickly my babies are growing up and how one day they will not need me the way they do now, how very soon they will get their own food and drinks and I will feel lost. Something that filled most of my day will be gone. I will long for them to need me for something and yet they will do it themselves or they will turn to their friends for the emotional support which they used to get from me. (Which I pray never happens)

So in order to be the best person and mom you can be you need time out, you need to rest. It will make you more physically and emotionally balanced. You're no good to your family as a stressed, burnt out nut case. So go rest!

BE HEALTHY

You need to eat right to function normally. Your body needs you to eat right for it to function normally as well. Breakfast, lunch and supper are essential to your body. You won't get fat if you eat the right foods! You can even snack throughout the day and you won't gain weight if you eat healthily. We have recently started the blood group diet, it helps that all four of us are the same blood group so cooking is easy. My children used to live on bread and all the bad foods, they always had digestive problems and other health issues. The amount of times I've had my children screaming with constipation is too many to count! It's the worst feeling seeing your child in pain and not being able to help them. Since we have started this diet, both my children favour vegetables over burgers, (this was not easy but staying strong in what is right has prevailed) they have no health problems, both are the healthiest they've ever been and even my husband and I have never felt better. I used to suffer from anemia, I was tired all day, every day; since changing our diet I am only tired if I don't get enough sleep. Having a healthy diet prolongs your life, makes you happier and gives you more energy and the best part is if your children see your healthy eating habits, it will set an example and good lifestyle for them. I'm not saying don't ever eat sweets or chocolates or ice cream but I'm saying limit them, enjoy them as they should be, a treat, not a meal replacement. Being healthy is a lifestyle, it's not only the food you eat, it's bathing daily, brushing your teeth and hair, taking vitamins and being fit. You're probably thinking, who doesn't do that? I'll never forget a post I saw on a social media site, a mom was saying how her 10 month old child seemed to need her all the time and she had to do housework and cook and keep order in the home. She was saying how bathing is a luxury and some days she just can't do it. Some were disgusted that she would skip a bath, and in any normal life it's unnatural to skip this simple, vital routine; but I knew where this poor tired mom was coming from, I was in the same situation. With a baby that feeds all day and all night, in between housework and maintaining a healthy relationship with your spouse, at the end of it all you are so tired that all you can do is fall into bed, running a bath is too much work when you only manage to get your big toe in and your baby starts crying. But it is vital for us to press on. Our children are small for such a short time and this too shall pass. All these seemingly normal things that we sometimes miss are important. With being a stay at home mom, I know, there are days I don't brush my hair, no one will see me and I have so much to do, I don't even remember. Any of you ever feel like that? We don't realize we are showing our kids that we don't need to maintain personal hygiene and healthy daily living.

Be the best you, be a Christ filled, healthy, purpose driven mom with balance and faith. Lead by example, your children watch how you behave and learn from you. Cultivate a new generation, not one that conforms to the sinful pleasures of the world but one who is content with what they have even if it is nothing. Teach good morals and discipline and love. The only way to do that is to implement it in your own life. Teach them that the importance of something isn't based on its price tag but rather its purpose. You affect people all around you on a daily basis, what do you want them to say about you when they have walked away?

The day I married my best friend

9 May 2009

CHAPTER 2

Cultivate your marriage

Before you get married, you need to be sure that you are
wholly committed to your husband. If there are other
men in your life who could drive a wedge between you
and your husband, you need to cut them off. Your
marriage comes before your friends. I don't mean you
need to turn away all your friends and start anew but for
instance, whilst I was growing up, majority of my friends
were boys, this is no problem whilst you're young and
naïve but as we get older and turn into young women,
those boys turn into young men. The things that young
boys wanted from young girls all of a sudden change and
the things men want from women become more intense.
Even one of my closest friends, who was like a brother to
me, told me after I got engaged that I couldn't get
married because he loved me. It was such a hard
decision, I had so many good memories with this man
and loved him as a best friend, but he was driving a
wedge between my fiancé and me. I had to make the
decision to cut off my friendship so as to preserve my
relationship and marriage. My husband and I decided in
the beginning until we had grown into our marriage with
trust and respect and a greater love than either of us had
ever known, to temporarily disengage friendships with
singles of the opposite sex. I avoided any single male
friends I had and he any female friends. We never cut
them off but slowly distanced ourselves so that there
was no interference in our marriage. The Bible tells us to
leave our parents and cleave to our spouses when we get

married, why then would we not do the same with our friends. Put your husband first in every decision of your life as God has instructed us to do so.

A marriage bound by Christ, with Christ at the center, the center of every decision, the center of what movies you watch, the center of the friendships you keep, the center of the way you treat one another and those around you, is the only way a marriage will sustain lifelong trials. You and your husband need to be evenly yoked. (2 Corinthians 6:14) No, not "yolked" like the egg, yoked as in oxen that carry a yoke around their neck. If one of the oxen are not yoked the same, they will not be able to move forward together. As a child I'm sure you did a three legged race where you tied your one leg to a friend's corresponding leg and tried to run a race. Imagine tying your leg to someone in this way but then also tying a short rope between your legs and a long rope between their legs. I'm certain you would be unsuccessful in moving forward with that person, if you did you would move very slowly and stop and fall along the way. This is what the Bible refers to about being unevenly yoked. Not only in religion, although this is the greatest way that we need to be evenly yoked, but also in decisions. You need to be evenly yoked with discipline over your children and with where you stand in your walk with God. You need to be in agreement basically on life's most vital decisions yet also the smallest ones. You and your spouse should never have different religious beliefs. If you cannot agree on those then everything else will become impossible to agree on. Your marriage may last for a while but if you are unevenly yoked in any area of your life there is a chance it will not last a lifetime.

Personally I do not agree with divorce, nor does the Bible, (Malachi 2:16 "I hate divorce," says the Lord, the God of Israel, "because the man who divorces his wife covers his garment with violence,") however there are some severe situations where I would agree it would be best for a couple, and some biblical reasons which could be grounds for divorce. "Falling out of love" is not a reason for divorce, nor if your husband spends too much time at work instead of with you, because he is supporting you financially, or many of the other petty reasons that people can find to live without their spouses and end their marriage. A marriage is a lifelong commitment, a covenant before God, if something is broken, don't throw it away... fix it. If your marriage is built around Christ however, then there will never be this consideration.

The most important thing, second to, or rather in part of a Christ centered marriage, is knowing your place in your marriage.

SUBMIT

Ephesians 5:22-27 "Wives, submit yourselves to your own husbands as you do to the Lord. For the husband is the head of the wife as Christ is the head of the church, so also wives should submit to their husbands in everything.

Husbands love your wives, just as Christ loved the church and gave himself up for her to make her holy, cleansing her by washing with water through the word, and to present her to himself as a radiant church, without stain or wrinkle or any other blemish, but holy and blameless."

Your place in your marriage is submission, respect your husband's authority. Who wears the pants in your house? Do you or does your husband? Your husband is the rightful head of your home. No, you're not the neck. (As great as it would be sometimes) When a decision is to be made you should discuss it together, but ultimately the decision should be that of the husband. Being the head of the home, he is directly under God's authority and he should be listening to God before anyone else. Your husband should love God more than he loves you because God's word says, love your wives the way God loves the church. If your husband loves God more than you, he will love you more than you would ever require. He will put you first in all his decisions and make sacrifices for the wellbeing of his family. If he is truly under the authority of God, he may sometimes make decisions that you think to yourself, seriously…. SERIOUSLY! But if God has breathed life into his decision, although you don't understand it, God will direct your footsteps. If your husband one day came home and said to you, "I feel God is telling us to sell everything we own and move to an igloo in Alaska." That would be one of those SERIOUSLY responses right? If my husband ever came home and told me that, I'd be terrified but I would do as he said. If God's will is to take us to Alaska to an igloo in the ice, who do I think I am to get in the way? My purpose is to glorify God, to have faith, to do God's will and to speak of God's goodness in my life. God may need you in Alaska, He wouldn't call you there without a reason. It may be difficult, there may be a war happening there, there may be no food, there will certainly be no shortage of water but you get the point. It may not be easy and you may feel like going is a death wish, but God sees the bigger picture, He knows His plan. He may take you to Alaska to allow your paths to cross with someone who can within a couple of hours send you back on a plane to carry out God's will of preaching to the nations in Afghanistan or Canada or England. We only see the first step placed in front of us but if we put our faith in God, He will set our footsteps in the right direction. God will always speak to your husband first and then set a confirmation upon your heart; a peace within you. Listen to your husband when God speaks to him. Be submissive. Why would your husband want to take his family to a new scary place? Would he seriously suggest something like that out of his own? God likes to take us out of our comfort zone. It grows us, strengthens us, and prepares us for life. We should never look at trials as a negative thing but rather as a lesson.

Let me share a portion of our testimony. After a few discouraging events in our life; God spoke to my husband. He came home from work one day and said to me, "God has told me that our season here has ended." I was terrified, I had always lived within at least half an hour drive of my mother and leaving my comfort zone terrified me. Even though I had a fear of the unknown, I stood by and supported my husband in this word from God. Wherever he chose to go I would follow because we would be in God's will for our life. When you get married it is no longer God's will for *your* life as an individual, you and your husband become one and that is why being evenly yoked is so crucial to sustaining a marriage. The next day, my husband came home from work and told me he had resigned. I'm sure the shock, gasp, horror was written all over my face. I quietly listened to him telling me how God had spoken to him and told him one thing, "Now, the time is now!" And so in obedience he handed in his one month notice. We had no plan, no new job lined up, at the end of the month we would be homeless with no income, a 2 year old child and a newborn baby. God gave him a picture of Peter who took a leap of faith and stepped out onto the water, and so we did the same. We didn't have a plan, but because we had been obedient to God we knew He would be faithful and He had a plan.

We placed our lives in God's hands and took a leap, a huge leap, of faith in God's will. The next day, my husband contacted his sister and told her all that God had been working in him. He told her he had resigned and had no plan, only to go where God leads us. She responded to him, "Yesterday at work we had a meeting and they are looking for someone to do bookings and marketing for the helicopter tours in our other branch in the Drakensberg…"

I was excited and terrified. All new to me, moving to a place where we knew no one, even my sister-in-law was an hour drive away from where we would be. I would have *NO ONE* except my husband and my two children. I was going to a new place where it snowed in Winter and was scorching hot in summer, to the mountains and away from the sea! OH MY GOSH! We went up to the Berg, my husband went for the interview and secured the position on the spot. He was to start work as soon as his notice was complete. We were set to move on the 1st of December, except, December is holiday season and everywhere was being rented for holiday purposes. So God provided a job where we seemingly, in just 2 weeks, we would be homeless. A week before we were to move, my sister-in-law found us a cottage. God came through at the last hour as per usual. That move was the best thing that ever happened to our family! It opened our eyes in so many ways and allowed us time alone to grow as a family. It put my husband in a job where he had to get into a helicopter almost daily, when he was previously terrified of flying. It took me away from my family and friends, completely out of our comfort zone, where we had no one to rely on besides God and one another. People were placed in our path, some to help us grow and some for us to help them grow. Our greatest life changing experience was shortly after moving to the berg. We were involved in a car accident that police called, "A miracle we survived", yet we all climbed out and walked away from the vehicle after rolling five times down a mountain side. I thank God daily for that accident. It reminds me every day that our God has a bigger plan for us, that we are not done on this earth because we have not completed the task God has set before us. It has given us an incredible testimony, one that I will never stop sharing, and I am so blessed and thankful that Jesus was in the car with us that day whilst we were singing His praise.

Being submissive to my husband when he heard from God was the best decision ever. Had we not gone to the Berg, had I said no I don't want to go, we would've missed out on so much. It is not always easy to deny ourselves and to follow God when we think we know better but if you're obedient to God's word and submit to your husband, God knows what is best for you.

COMPROMISE AND COMMUNICATE

Genesis 2:18 The Lord God said, "It is not good for the man to be alone. I will make a helper suitable for him." Romans 15:5-6 "May the God who gives endurance and encouragement give you a spirit of unity among yourselves as you follow Christ Jesus, so that with one heart and mouth you may glorify the God and the Father of our Lord Jesus Christ!" Our marriage should also bring glory to God daily in the way we treat our husbands, in the way we speak to them, help them, respect them and love them.

There are so many incredible scriptures on marriage, it is so hard to choose which to include, thankfully God left His word and enclosed all wisdom into marriage. I encourage you to read your Bible if you are going through a trial in your marriage, there are such incredible little nuggets of life and love in the Bible. All the answers are in there.

As I've said before, when you get married you become one. It's no longer my life and your life, it's our life. Do things together, take joy in what makes your husband happy, even if you do not participate. For the first few years of our marriage, (we were still very young then) my husband loved to play paintball, I used to take my book and go with him once a week. I used to sit and read whilst he and a group played paintball at an abandoned building on a farm. Whilst reading, I would occasionally glance up from my book and see the boys running for their lives and see the excitement on my husband's face as he sat afterwards telling me all that happened during the game... Paintball wasn't *my* thing, but because it made my husband happy, I too shared in his joy. In the same respect, riding horses is not my husband's thing either, yet he would come with me and sit and watch whilst I rode and listen to me afterwards, telling, him about how horses and humans have such strong connections. Looking back I have to giggle. This is the whole thing though, we may not share the same interests but we need to share in the things that bring joy to our significant other.

Compromise so that you can find a place where both of you are happy. It's not a game of tit for tat but rather wanting to do something because it makes your spouse happy. On a weekend, the whole weekend doesn't need to be selfishly absorbed by one person's wants. There are weekends when my husband wants to go wave skiing and the weather is perfect, yet I have agreed to have coffee at home with our friends. We compromise, we either ask our friends to please join us at the beach and come back to our place for coffee afterwards, or we wait until after our coffee date to go to the beach. If we don't get to go that day I make sure that we go the next day, so we both get to enjoy our weekend. There has to be compromise in a marriage, without it we start to live as individuals, and start living past one another, and then before you know it, you are two single people who just live in the same house with completely separate lives. I am thankful I have never had to live through that, however I have had friends who have been through this, some realized in time to fix it where others unfortunately just didn't end up with a lasting marriage.

Communication is equally as important. Men find it very hard to do this purely because they just expect us to know certain things. My husband once said to me, "I'm sorry I didn't tell you I expected you to just know." At first I was most annoyed and thought out loud, "How can you expect me to read your mind?" My husband response stirred something in me, "Because you know me so well and I see you as a part of myself, I forget that you are a separate individual. I expect because I know, that you would know." This is what it should be like, but we need to communicate in order to read their minds. Our lives are so busy that we need to make time to speak to one another.

As our children start to find their voices this becomes increasingly more difficult. In our home, we try to choose a time when our children are occupied to chat together. This is not always very successful; the moment one of us starts to speak our children will inevitably come into the room and ask for something. And children do not hear that you are already speaking. I am trying with all I have to teach my children to HEAR and to listen, and to wait their turn to speak. My daughter will walk into the kitchen where we are speaking, hear we are talking, and without missing a beat or batting an eyelid, she chimes in over us, "Mom I need....." It's inevitable. We cannot get angry with them, they aren't doing it intentionally, they are learning and they are children but there is nothing more frustrating than trying to have a conversation whilst your children are awake! Keep the important conversations for when your children are asleep, when you can give your husband your undivided attention. Leave your phone alone, don't look at the TV whilst he's speaking to you, I realize it is your favourite show, they're all your favourites right? Switch everything off and truly listen to your husband. Speak about things of importance; speak about his day at work and your day at home. Try not to moan about how tough it was with the kids all day, be supportive if he has had a terrible day at work and if you are blessed to be able to stay home with your children, then be appreciative of the fact that he goes to work daily to provide for you, as the Bible commands, so that you are able to be at home with your children.

Communication is vital to sustain any relationship, it not only keeps you in the loop with what is going on with one another but it builds trust in one another. One day when you are old and your children have all moved out, communication will be the core of your marriage. My mother in law, on my wedding day, said to me, "Never go to bed angry with one another, even if you have to stay awake all night to resolve your problem, never go to bed angry with one another." This was such a crucial piece of advice that I have used throughout our, so far, seven years of marriage. If you have good communication in your marriage, then your marriage is built upon a solid foundation.

PRAY TOGETHER

Another key piece of advice which has proven to be true countless times in our marriage is, "A family that prays together, stays together." We pray a blessing and give thanksgiving at every meal, altogether, as a family. Every night, at our children's bed time, we lie in bed together and pray as a family. There have been times when my husband was working a second job in the evenings as well as working during the day. During these times he was not with us for bedtime prayers and I can honestly say, the effects of not being able to spend time in God's presence as a family was felt. Needless to say, night time working soon came to an end. Our family relationship was much more important than our financial situation. Besides, when we spent time together in prayer as a family, God resolved our financial situation. Praying together is the number one key that bonds your family in the spiritual as well as on this earth.

Pray not only as a family but with your husband alone. Pray about your country, its leaders, pray for your church, thank God for His constant hand of protection that has kept you safe daily. Thank him for your marriage, your husband and your children. Ask him to guide you in teaching your children with love and discipline and in maintaining a healthy balance of both, so that you can raise your children to walk as Christ walked. Ask and thank God for daily refining you, teaching you, for His sacrifice of Jesus. Commit your finances to God, your children, your marriage, whatever situation you are requiring an answer for. Give it all to God in prayer, together. And stand in agreement with one another. Don't be discouraged if God doesn't answer you immediately. His timing is always perfect and it's not always our timing. Be willing to do whatever God asks of you as a family.

Besides praying as a family and praying with your husband alone, you NEED to spend time alone, by yourself, without your husband, without your kids, without your phone or TV or computer, JUST YOU; alone with God, with your Bible and pray. This goes back again to Chapter 1 but I cannot express the importance of praying. Praying is also a part of communication, not with your husband, but with God. Yes, God knows your heart, but He wants more than to listen to your heart, he wants a relationship with you; to communicate with you. Just as you know your husband, you know if he is angry or happy, but you still wish to talk to him. Imagine your husband never spoke to you. He showed you he loved you by doing considerate things, like bringing flowers home for you, but imagine he just handed them to you and said nothing, EVER! Would that not be hurtful? It is the same in our relationship with God, he knows our hearts, our good works show our love for him, BUT He wants to hear from us and He wants to speak to us. He longs for that intimate relationship that we too often deprive him of. We are his children, I would hate for my children to never speak to me. So spend time in prayer, as a couple, as a family and alone with God. Set the foundation for your family.

Rest in God

CHAPTER 3

Cultivate your pre-pregnancy

Perhaps you have chosen to buy this book because you want to become a mom. You are trying to fall pregnant or perhaps you are trying for baby two or three or four or golly, I can't wrap my brain around more than two precious blessings. For those of you with a big family, good for you!

Your pre-pregnancy part of life is as important as your pregnancy. This is where being unevenly yoked, communication and prayer *all* come into play. Make sure having this baby is something both you and your husband want. Something you're ready for because if you cannot afford to currently live, then having a baby would be irresponsible.

I don't say you need to have a heap of money piled up somewhere, however you need to have enough money to be able to put a roof over your heads, have groceries and fuel and medication if it is required; basically as a couple you should be self-sustained, not dependent on others for your survival or finances. If you are supporting yourselves yet still feel you are waiting to have more than enough money and that is what's stopping you, then get over it. You will *never* have a baby if you are waiting to be financially ready. If you both want a baby badly enough you will always make a plan, you will be more than happy to sacrifice luxuries to accommodate the cost of your precious new joy.

Before my husband and I started our baby journey, we agreed that it would be more beneficial to our family for me to not go back to work after our baby was born, rather than to earn a salary small enough to pay for our petrol to and from work and daycare fees. If God would entrust *me* with a precious soul, I owe it to Him to raise my child myself; besides the fact that I so badly wanted to be a Mom in every sense of the word.

When I fell pregnant with my daughter, my husband and I were both working full time, earning salaries and yet we were swamped with debt. We wanted all the new clothes, cellphones, gaming devices etc. We had just had to buy a new car too which we were paying on top of medical aid bills, never mind our standard monthly living expenses but we were coping. When our daughter was born and I was no longer employed, by the grace of God and faith we made it. People helped us, God blessed me with people to teach me skills I was lacking in - photography, and God helped me to grow my photography business. Even through my business though, I never miss an opportunity to share our many testimonies of God's goodness. I'm not giving free reign to anyone who says, "I want a baby so I'll have one regardless of whether we can afford one it or not." There's responsible and irresponsible.

Having a baby should be a decision made AFTER marriage. I am so saddened when I hear of babies being born before marriage, and hearing, "But we love one another." How many of those people ever end up married? A man generally wouldn't buy the cow when he is already getting the milk for free. And when you have a baby before your man has committed to you in the eyes of God, he generally feels pressured to marry you. When a commitment is made from pressure and not readiness, it is very rarely successful. A small, tiny, minute percentage of those couples end up married and happy. God destined us to get married and then have children, and to take neither marriage, nor having a baby lightly. Wanting a baby because your friends' baby is so cute and you just have to have one, is irresponsible. Having sex before marriage is irresponsible; the Bible says, if you cannot abstain from sex be married. If you love your partner and he loves you there should be no reason you wouldn't want to get married. Sex used to be a sacred act to consummate your marriage, to bind your soul to your husbands and in saying your body is no longer yours, it belongs to your husband. How many people own the rights to a part of your soul and body? Having a baby with an ex who couldn't commit to marriage makes life difficult for everyone involved, you, your new partner or husband, the families, your ex, but the person it affects the most, throughout their entire life, is your child.

Being responsible in making the decision to have a baby should at least have a few things to your checklist. Married? Living alone with your husband in your own place, whether owned or rented that you are paying for? Does he have a secure job, one that he doesn't plan on leaving without first finding a more suitable position? Are you living a healthy lifestyle? If you have a baby will it make you homeless or will you not afford to feed your family? Are you ready to give up partying and drinking to be a responsible mother? In this respect I can say if any of the answers are "No" you are not ready to consider having a baby. Be responsible about your decision. A baby is a life changing decision. I always said, if there are things you still want to do where your baby cannot go with you, then you're not ready for a baby! There is nothing I do that my children couldn't do or go with me. They are the biggest part of my life, why would I exclude them? Everyone said to us, having a baby changes your life, you can't do the things you used to; as though a baby holds you back in life. If you are not ready for a baby then yes, your baby will hold you back in life. We didn't have to give up a hefty social life full of partying, drinking etc. We were already the couple whose idea of a good time was going for coffee with a few friends. Our baby just brought added joy to our life and made our life complete.

If you are ready for a baby, your checklist is in order and you want to earn that title of mom; yet you can't seem to fall pregnant. If you're trying for a baby; stop! My husband and I made a decision to "try" for a baby. Well, let me tell you, if it is not God's timing, then no matter how hard you "try", you will not succeed. I am so thankful for this fact. Our months of trying proved futile and one day our car died; *really* died, like the engine dropped out died! I was so thankful that I hadn't fallen pregnant, I know God can do anything but perhaps the financial strain of a new baby and a new car would've caused me to lose my baby. This would've crushed me. Looking back we would never have afforded our new car and a newborn baby. Thank God that His plan and His timing is perfect! 8 months later we decided we were now "ready" for a baby.

"Trying" for a baby is too stressful, it makes your sexual relationship turn into a baby making chore; the added pressure on both you and your husband prevents you from conceiving. So we decided not to try, we would simply just let be what was meant to be when the time was right. We didn't think that same month would be God's timing. 3 weeks later I found out I was pregnant with my first child.

When in your pre-pregnant phase, you and your husband need to be on the same page with your wants with regards to a baby, if one is not on board it should not be considered. If you both want a baby then faith and prayer are the only tools you need. Be patient, our timing is not always God's timing, but He has good reason for that. When the time is right, your pre-pregnancy phase will come to an end and a little life will begin to grow when you fall pregnant. I pray God's timing and blessing over your pregnancy when you get to that road in your life. May you be blessed during this part of your journey into motherhood.

The beginning of a mothers love

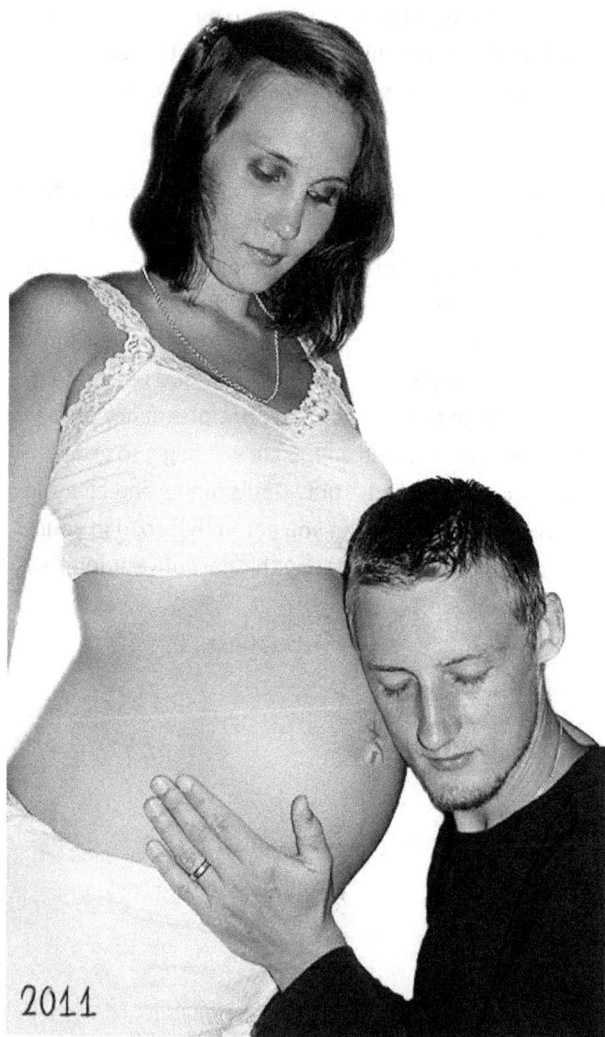

2011

CHAPTER 4

Cultivate your pregnancy

Congratulations on your pregnancy. I pray God blesses your child, that he or she will form part of a great generation and will bring change, and let their light shine that the world sees Christ through them when they look at them. I pray God's hand upon you and your child throughout your pregnancy, that everything goes smoothly, that there are no complications unless God's greater will destines it so for the wellbeing of you and your child.

I pray God's hand over your marriage, that He will be the glue to bind the two of you together if there are times that you face trials. I thank God for blessing you with this child and pray that He will guide you in raising your child to live a life pleasing to God. I thank God for the gift of life, not only the life that is gently forming perfectly in your womb, but the gift of our eternal life that we have received because of Jesus' sacrifice. Thank you Father for this couple that is about to grow from just husband and wife to a little family, thank You that this child will strengthen the bond not only of mother and child but also of husband and wife. In Jesus name I pray. Amen.

Now marks the beginning of a new journey for you and your husband. You will most likely experience many feelings and emotions during your pregnancy. Joy, exhaustion, fear, immobilizing nausea, back pain, heartburn, reflux, pain in your ribs, butterflies in your tummy, hard shoves and pushes of a tiny person trying to break through your belly, so many different ones and not necessarily all of them. My worst was the number of times I had to tinkle in the space of one hour; having to pinch my legs together whenever I sneezed so I didn't wet myself. The joys of pregnancy, right?

The best feeling of all is the maternal feeling. The, "I'm a Mommy," feeling. The, "I'm having a baby," feeling. When I fell pregnant I couldn't wait to tell EVERYONE! I'm sure I told some people twice because I couldn't remember who I had told. Shame those poor people. I was so thankful to finally have a little life growing inside of me and I was so proud that God had chosen me, and entrusted me with this beautiful gift.

My first pregnancy was tough I'm not going to lie. I couldn't eat red meat throughout my whole pregnancy without bringing it back up within the hour. I suffered with terrible acid reflux, my baby got her foot stuck under my ribs several times which is extremely painful... however, I said to my husband before I fell pregnant (I really wanted a baby), "I welcome the morning sickness, the backache, all the symptoms, I welcome them all because it means I will have a little life growing inside of me!" Let me tell you, even through all my moaning, pushing my husband aside for 3 months, unintentionally, I was so sick I couldn't handle being too close to anyone, pain, lack of sleep, my terrible 25 hour labour, through it all, I had such a maternal love for my unborn child.

I spoke to her constantly. When we did praise and worship at church I couldn't help but hold my tummy, my precious baby, and sing praises to God for this true blessing. Once I got over the morning sickness and was feeling a bit more human, I included my husband in everything. He was as much a part of my pregnancy as I was. He was at every scan, he felt my belly move, he was so supportive even though it was frustrating throughout the morning sickness months. He was my rock all throughout my pregnancy and he loved our baby just as much as I did, he used to talk to her and play his guitar for her... a dad was formed in him from the moment we saw that little flicker of a heartbeat for the first time.

So how do you cultivate your pregnancy?

Never stop thanking God. Not every woman gets the opportunity to bear their own child. I have many friends who have lost babies or not been able to even fall pregnant. This is not because God doesn't trust them with their own children, He knows they are needed for a greater purpose. God has given us free will in life, some women for whatever reason, feel that they cannot look after their children and either abandon them or give them up for adoption and sadly some children are orphaned after losing parents.

God chose those unable to have their own children, to give a loving home to a child who was abandoned or orphaned; a child whose parents cannot be there for them. These parents have such love that they can love someone else's child as their own. This is much more difficult than having your own child, it is by no means easy but this is why God chose these special people for this. It takes a special kind of woman to be able to do this, to be able to look past that child's history, look past their flaws and take on the challenge of molding a sometimes undisciplined, broken child into a beautifully matured Christ loving individual. I am blessed to know one of these incredible moms and have watched her journey and watched her grow from strength to strength, she has become a completely different person. She has such a love for her daughter and her daughter for her. She has raised her child into an incredible daughter of God, with strong values and a heart of love and kindness. Both her and her daughter are truly blessed and a blessing to all they meet. This love is cultivated when you meet your child for the first time but is just as strong as that of a mom who bears their own child.

Having your own baby however, creates a different, special bond between mother and child. It is God's gift specifically to a woman; I so often wished my husband could feel from the inside what it felt like but God gave this special gift to us ladies. This is a true honour that you have been blessed with. Give thanks daily!

As in chapter 1, but this time it's vitally important, not only for your life but for that of your baby. Rest! Take it easy! I'm not saying be lazy but don't overdo it, be cautious with doing strenuous activities, listen to your doctor and more importantly LISTEN TO YOUR BODY! If your body says, "time-out", take it! You need it, and the well-being of your baby needs it.

Don't feel bad to ask for help. I am a super independent person, if something needs to be done, I want to be able to do it, not have to wait for someone to come and do it for me. You can be superwoman once your baby is born, during your pregnancy ask for help if you need it, and accept it. Don't stop doing everything, if you do, you're going to gain weight and will have a tough time losing it after your baby is born. Stay active without going overboard. Go for walks with your husband. Swim… swimming is probably the best exercise you can do because your body weight is supported by the water. Please don't hold your breath under water, I really wouldn't suggest that, but swim, swim, swim.

Keep a healthy diet. You are eating for two but you do not need to eat double. Taking a prenatal vitamin helps to give you and your baby the added nutrients you need. Folic acid and calcium are really important while pregnant and during breastfeeding too. If you eat the same as you did before you were pregnant your baby will still get the nutrients they need provided you are eating right. Vegetables, fruit, fruit juice, LOTS of water, ask your doctor which foods to avoid, for example some say tuna due to the high levels of mercury which is said to be very bad for the development of your growing baby's brain. If you get hungry in between breakfast, lunch and supper, which you most likely will, don't starve yourself. That is not beneficial to you or your baby. When you get snack attack cravings, don't eat junk, eat fruit, nuts, yoghurt, vegetables, chicken salads, healthy food. Not only will it help you to not gain much weight but it will make you and your baby healthy. I am not a qualified dietician or doctor but I did a lot of studies in nutrition and can tell you even from my own experience, how eating right makes such a difference, not only in your pregnancy but in your life in general.

Praise God, eat right and keep a healthy lifestyle, rest and enjoy your pregnancy… Not so hard right. Your pregnancy will be over before you know it. Take joy in the good and bad during your pregnancy, you can't just pull out a "preggie" snapshot once baby is born and feel those kicks just by looking at a photograph. When your baby is born and pregnancy ends, it's finished. Enjoy it while it lasts! May your pregnancy and the arrival of your beautiful gift be smooth and a blessed time in your journey.

Zoë Elissa

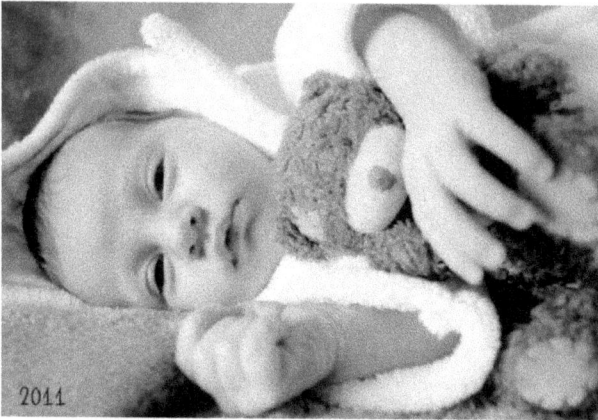

Zoë meaning "Life"

Born on 24th April 2011,

Easter Sunday

CHAPTER 5

Cultivate your first child

Congratulations on the precious blessing of your first child. Whether you have chosen to bottle or breastfeed your baby, is up to you. Breastfeeding is definitely better but you are no less of a mom if you bottle feed than if you breastfeed. With my daughter I so badly wanted to breastfeed, and I did for a few weeks but when I stopped because I thought I didn't have enough milk, I sobbed, I felt like such a failure as a mother because that was what God created us to do. That is such a minor part of your child's development and it does not affect what type of mother you are. My daughter and I have such a strong bond regardless of the fact that I didn't breastfeed her as long as I did with my son.

When you have a baby, everyone becomes a doctor and psychiatrist. Just smile and nod and take the part of advice that you need, what worked for someone else will not necessarily work for you.

Throughout the rest of your life your child will bring you joy, laughter, rebellion, anger and frustration, but most importantly, love! From birth, cultivate your child to be a loving, disciplined, friendly and God loving individual. Raise them to walk in Christ, even if this is the only thing you can teach your child, it is the only thing they will need.

No matter what your child does, God has formed a love and a bond so deep within us, that we will never stop loving them. Your child is the greatest gift you will ever receive from anyone, whether your child is perfect or has a disability, no mother would dispute that their child makes their life complete. Even the mothers who have had miscarriages, or lost their children after birth, will tell you that their child was the best thing that ever happened to them. If you are one of those moms who have lost a child, my heart and sincere condolences go out to you. I pray God continues to heal your heart and make it whole.

Now your new little bundle has been born, you are about to embark on a new, lifelong journey. How exciting!! More like, how terrifying! It's ok, you've got this, God has given you a manual of instructions, you cannot access them all at once but I can promise you that when you need them, you will know them. Always follow your heart. God has given us a mother instinct that kicks in whenever we need it. People always used to say to me, "You are her mommy, you will know what to do."

Only when I had my first challenge with my first born precious daughter, did I understand. Somehow, I just naturally knew what I had to do. God has given us this natural blessing, the gift of a mother's sense. Having your baby at home, the first few days… weeks… scratch that, the first 3 months, is the hardest. I always say to the mommies who bring their baby's for their first newborn photos, if you can get through the first 3 months then you've done it!

My second day at hospital, after my daughter was born, the doctor gave me the ok to take my baby home. GO

HOME! Are you crazy! Who will I call if something is wrong? I don't want to go home! There's no nurse at home! So although I was given the all clear I decided to stay another night. I have to laugh when I think of my son's 4 hour labour and quick and easy birth compared to my daughters. I wanted to leave immediately after my son was born but managed to get out after 9 hours, it would've been sooner had he not been born at 1am. Yet, with my daughter, I wouldn't leave; this new tiny little bundle terrified me with all her tininess and fragility.

When I was getting ready to leave the hospital, I was changing her into her going home outfit, she *had* to have one of those, but she seemed so tiny, so fragile, I was so afraid I would hurt or break her. I called for the nurse, and in walked this little women who just whipped off my baby girls outfit, pulled her little arms through her vest and pulled on her onesie. Gosh, it would've taken me all day to do that had I not seen how rough and tough these little ones really are.

It was so amazing being at home with my husband and my little girl that day, until we tried to sleep that night. Every little sound my princess made I jumped out of bed to check if she was choking or struggling to breathe. Maybe it's just me, but as a first time mom, I was paranoid. I would never forgive myself if I didn't check and something was wrong. Needless to say I didn't get much sleep that night, nor the second, or third or first week.

As our babies get older, we learn what their little noises mean, what emotions they are experiencing by moans or gurgles, what they need when they cry. God has equipped us to know! If you put your child before yourself in everything you do, you are a fantastic mother!

Don't feel bad if you think you seem paranoid or over protective, despite many people's theories of spoiling your child, I disagree. You love your child enough and you're not afraid to show them. There are so many different theories of being overprotective and spoiling your children. In my opinion, each child is different and so is each mother. You need to have a balance.

I am an over protective, control freak mother but I firmly believe in boundaries and discipline. There are 2 ways to spoil a child. One way you create a spoilt brat, the other is a child who loves people and has respect for those around them and for life.

The first way to spoil a child is to love them by buying their love and affection but pushing them aside so that you can live your life without the burden of your children being around all the time. If you want to enjoy life and constantly give your child to someone to "babysit" so that you can have that girl's night out or visit friends or go shopping. Don't get me wrong there's nothing wrong with doing those things but your baby can go with you if you're being a responsible individual and living for Christ. It's no easy task but it's a sacrifice you make.

If your child spends more time with someone other than you (excluding school times) in the times that you are not at work yourself, then I'm sorry but you're doing it wrong. Harsh maybe? Had God wanted your mother, your friend, your aunties, uncles, brothers, sister's wife to raise your child, He would've given that child to them. GOD CHOSE YOU!

What is more important to you, your baby learning independence and growing up to be insecure or your child being maybe a little dependent on you whilst they are young, but being secure and growing up to know that no matter what you will always be there.

The other way to spoil your child is to love, love, love them; to not feel guilty to have them in your bed or to not feel guilty to lie with your baby or rock them to sleep. To breastfeed your baby until age 2, to bath with your baby until they get too big, to carry your baby until they're a child and your back can no longer cope with it, to sacrifice the irresponsible life you used to lead to become a responsible mother.

Humanity, researchers, whatever you'd like to call them, in my opinion, have become soft with what it means to be a mom. Nowadays all the articles I read are how to make a mom's life easier. Don't rock your child because you'll have to do it forever. How long is forever, seriously. When your child gets to an age where they can understand what you say to them (between a year to 2 years) you would not still be rocking them. Children change, baby's preference changes. When my first was still a baby, other moms frowned upon me because I lay by my child every time she was to sleep. I would get comments like, "Your child is going to be dependent on you," or, "how long are you going to do that?" or my personal favourite, "It would be so much easier for you to just put your baby down and let her cry herself to sleep, she would only do it a few times then she would get it…"

REALLY! Why don't you move to another country where you have no one, get a room mate, someone you don't know and go to your room by yourself and cry yourself to sleep, while everything you know is on the other side of the world. Imagine this tiny little life you've just brought into the world, they don't know you, only by your voice, they don't know where they are, what different sounds and smells are, how terrified they must be if you put them by themselves in a room, close the door so they can't hear your voice, which makes the room dark except for shadows on the wall, which if you ask any child they will tell you how scary shadows are, and now you expect this tiny tot to be happy to go to sleep. The child is crying because they are scared, they want you because they feel safe when you are around.

Even when we had guests over, anyone can tell you, when it was bedtime I would excuse myself and my husband would continue to charm our guests, whilst I lay with my daughter until she fell asleep; even if it took 45 minutes. As they get older and start to understand you can explain about shadows and teach them there is nothing to be afraid of, if your child is raised in a Christian home, from the get go you can teach them never to fear anything because God is always with them.

My daughter is now nearly 5 and my son 2 and a half, I *still* lie with my children until they fall asleep. Not because I have to, but because I want to. It's not a burden for me to know my children feel safe, they feel secure and protected and loved. Besides that it is the one time of the day when they aren't running around and I don't have to chase them for a cuddle without them running away to go and play. I can hug and kiss them and sing softly to them or whisper sweetly how much I love them. I usually pray softly whilst they are falling asleep, I whisper a prayer of thanksgiving of how thankful I am for my incredible blessings, how thankful I am for their beautiful hearts and how they have love for EVERYONE. If this world was a safe place and there was no such thing as stranger danger I am certain my children would bring everyone they meet to the feet of Jesus. Their innocence, their complete love for people reminds me of the love of our Father; so unconditional and pure.

Which way would you rather spoil your children? I am not saying that putting your child in their own room and own bed is wrong, but if your baby cries and is scared then in your own opinion does it seem right to leave them there to cry until they eventually fall asleep? Some moms are built to be able to do that, I am not by any means trying to judge or convict anyone out there, but I am saying that spoiling your children with love is not wrong.

Our children are at home, if we are lucky, for 18 years of our life. 18 YEARS OF YOUR WHOLE LIFE! Would it really be so terrible to sacrifice 18 years of your life doting over your child?

I personally prefer the, spoil your child with love method, *however*, if you spoil your child with both love and buying everything their heart desires, you will end up with a spoilt brat, which no one likes. Discipline is the most important part of raising your child. Without it, you are teaching them they need only come to you when they want something and you will just get it for them. They need to know the word NO, that they have to work for things, that they need to have responsibility and that it's not ok to smack or scream or cry because they don't get their own way. Discipline is vital but goes hand in hand with understanding.

What people consider to be a "tantrum" is purely your child trying to learn to express their emotions. It's their way of saying, "I don't understand what I'm feeling, why can I not do that, why can I not have that toy, why must I go to bed when I'm not tired?"

Too many parents are too quick to try and stop their children from crying because they are having a meltdown after responding to something. Your children aren't born with the understanding of their emotions. They need to learn, firstly to identify each emotion, and then how to react to each emotion.

You are their teacher. If you are disciplining them by shouting or smacking or time out when they are young and still learning to identify their emotions then you are teaching them that they are not entitled to feel a response to whatever has happened. For instance if you are at the shops and your child takes a toy off the shelf, when you want to leave but not buy the toy and you take the toy away, your child cries and screams at the top of their lungs as though you're murdering them and the whole store turns to see what you've done, you terrible parent for making your child cry!

This has happened to me and I didn't even have my husband with me so I couldn't even pass my child along. Instead of giving your child a hiding out of embarrassment and for seeming like a bad parent for not "disciplining" you child, hold your baby, continue walking out the door even if your child is trying to free themselves from your arms, speak softly and gently to them, they will eventually quieten down to try to hear what you are saying. Keep repeating yourself quietly, explaining why you cannot buy the toy, because they have more toys than the shop itself, if you purchased every toy there would be none for the other children and it is good to share with others.

Explain to your child you understand they are upset and frustrated because they really did want that toy, but perhaps they might get it for their birthday or Christmas. When you tell your child what emotion they are experiencing it will help them to identify what they are feeling and why. You could even go as far as to tell them how there are even things you want but can't have because you cannot always have everything you want in life, that people have to work for things but that there are more important things in life than having everything money can buy. Teach them that the most important things in life are the things that cannot be bought. This is still discipline but it is disciplining with love and gentleness.

Before you get angry and decide on which method of discipline you're about to break out. Try to understand your child, why are they reacting like this? Are they tired because they missed a nap because you've been busy with them in town all day? If so is it fair to get angry with them when you are the reason they are tired and cannot tell you because they don't understand. Are they hungry or sick or thirsty? When our children are young, when they do not understand, we need to understand for them. They are only children, you were once where your child is and your parents had to teach you.

God blessed me with an incredible teacher; my mother has raised me into the person I am today, partially by herself, but also with the help of others along the way. She raised me with love, the most sacrificial and unconditional love that I have ever experienced and because of that, I have the tools to raise my children in this way. For this I am truly blessed and thankful.

There are times when your child is just not listening, they are being blatantly disobedient and trying to see how far they can push you, you need to find a discipline method that works for your family, discipline should be done with love though, never in anger; but discipline is vital in raising a child.

When people look at our children I don't want them to think, "What brats". So we teach our children to be loving, friendly, obedient individuals and that it's ok to have emotions and responses. Each child is different and each parent raises their child differently.

The way things have worked for me, may not work for everyone. I know for my family based on the parents we are and the way we raise our children, we have the happiest, balanced, Jesus filled children I know. You would only understand if you met them. My first child, my daughter, has such a beautiful heart. She is such a blessing to me that she is my first. She has made raising my son so much easier because he sees good behavior and love from her. We have taught her to teach her brother, to share with him and love him and to be his best friend.

When I was pregnant I was convinced I was having a boy the whole way through my pregnancy. We didn't find out our baby's gender until she was born. I so badly wanted a boy that I didn't even consider that it might not be. God knows what we need so when we sometimes don't get what we want, know that it's God giving you what you NEED instead. Had my daughter been born a boy it would've changed my life in so many ways. I would never have had a second baby if my little boy had come first because of the type of mother I am. Don't get me wrong, I love my son and have the most incredible bond with him, but any mother of a boy will tell you that boys are much more demanding than girls. My daughter is so independent yet my son in many ways, but not all, is so dependent. "Ma vas" is the term most used. Little boys have a true love and affection for their mommy which means mommy must be there... all the time.

Before my daughter was born we chose a name for a boy and a girl. Our little boy, I believed we were having, would have been Caleb. Our little girl would be Zoë

Elissa; both biblical names as a testimony to our Father's goodness for blessing us with our baby. Our baby was due on the 27th of April 2011, a Wednesday. God predestined my baby's birth to be a true testament. My baby girl, Zoë, meaning life, was born on the 24th April 2011, Easter Sunday; and such a true blessing to our family.

In conclusion, strive to teach your first child with love, patience, understanding and obedience, raise them to be kind and honest, teach them to not be hurtful, if they have nothing nice to say to then rather keep quiet, don't fret the small things, life is too short to get upset over insignificant things, teach them being in time is important and to always keep to their word. My mother always said to me, "If you make a plan with someone don't ever cancel it if something better comes along." That was the best piece of advice I was ever given. Teach them to listen to that still inner voice, "If in doubt, don't" my mom always used to say. There are many wise things my mom has taught me throughout the years, which have stuck; nuggets of good advice that I pass on to my children.

We cannot protect our children from evil their whole lives but whilst we can, we should, don't allow them to watch these evil, aggressive cartoons, don't tolerate harsh speaking and swearing, don't buy that toy that looks like it belongs in a horror movie just because all the other kids have them.

Raise your children with good morals and a loving, good heart; they set the example for all your children who follow.

Remember who came first,

don't push them aside

CHAPTER 6

Cultivate your first child during your second pregnancy

When I found out I was pregnant with my second child, I was so concerned. I was so in love with my daughter, she was perfect as she was. What if this second baby changed her, what if she felt pushed aside, discarded, *jealous*. I didn't want my precious angel to turn into a terror because of her sibling and as horrible as it may sound, I didn't want to share the bond I had with her, with another little girl. I didn't want her to feel like she had to compete for my attention or love.

I researched, spoke to moms and watched my friend's and family's children interacting. With much prayer for my child to remain as she was and to love me as much, if not more than she already did, I got it! If your child is included in everything and feels a part of your unborn child's life, they will love their sibling even more.

When I fell pregnant with my boy, Zoë was 19 months old. I told her she was going to have a brother or sister. As you can imagine she had no idea what I was telling her. I booked my first scan and we told her we were going to see her sibling in mommy's tummy. Although she couldn't really make out what she was looking at, we explained to her every time, and she would hug and kiss my tummy. When we found out we were having a boy, we told her she was having a brother, a little boy who would be her best friend. She would talk quietly to her brother in my tummy during the day, and I would constantly tell her that she is the most important person in his life and that she must teach him to be a good boy.

My daughter was at every scan, she felt my tummy move first, she was at part of my baby shower (she left with daddy a little way in because she wanted to be with him too), she helped me choose clothes for her little brother and some toys, she tested out his pram and car chair for him. She was in our maternity photoshoot, I did one with just her and I and we did a family shoot with an incredible photographer and friend, Zoë was included in EVERYTHING!

I loved having my baby girl at home with me all the time, she helped me to sand down and paint her brother's wooden cot and to get it ready with the pillows and linen. She helped me paint his changing station cupboard and pack away and unpack and repack away all his toiletries from the baby shower, several times. She helped to unwrap the presents and hang his new clothes out to dry before his arrival. She did absolutely everything with me.

During this hormonal, pregnant time, be careful not to take out your frustrations on your child.

I will never forget a time I was sorting through my baby boy's things, I had just put up his polystyrene name and tatty teddy bear, that was given to me for my baby shower, above his cot on the wall. I was so thrilled, it looked so beautiful. I went to the toilet for the umpteenth time that day and when I returned, I found my daughter standing in the cot ripping the name to pieces. I was so distraught I burst into tears asking why? Why did you break it? She stopped and also cried not understanding why I was crying and what she had done wrong! What was I doing? It was a polystyrene name, yet I was standing at the foot of the bed sobbing.

She didn't know, she was only 2 years old, she had never seen this thing before. She sobbed and sobbed as I held her which made me sob and sob. I was so upset that it had been broken but even more so that I had reacted this way. I had broken my rule, before you react consider why your child is doing this. Her lack of understanding accumulated with my lack of understanding and had us both in tears. My husband is a very wise soul, when I told him what had happened, he comforted me and said to me, "Always remember, what is more important to you, your possessions, or your relationships."

How often do we get angry or upset because our child has accidentally broken something? Our possessions can be replaced, but our children's tears cannot be taken back. The tongue is our most powerful weapon, we should speak love, not with antagonistic, harsh, anger filled words.

The only way your child will change towards you is if you change towards your child. Love them the same if not more, don't take out your hormonal rollercoaster on your child, cuddle them often telling them that even though you are having their sibling, that you will never stop loving them. If you do all this then you will have no problems when your second little bundle arrives. Only

you can cultivate your child to be ready for their little
brother or sister.

Judah Travis

Judah meaning "Praise to God"

Born on 22nd August 2013

CHAPTER 7

Cultivate your second, third, fourth… children

I am so thankful that I taught my first child to listen and love. It has made raising my second so much easier because he learns from her. Just because you have a second child to teach from scratch doesn't mean you can stop teaching your first though.

Now that your second baby is here, you're remembering how stressful it is to have a newborn but it's somehow a little easier this time, you're not quite as frazzled as before. This time you're able to maintain normal living… well kind of. With your second baby you can't do things quite the same as you did with your first because you have another child to consider as well.

What do you do if both need you at once? Your first should always take priority over your second child, provided it's not to your baby's detriment. If your baby is choking but you're changing your toddler's nappy, you wouldn't carry on with your toddler leaving your baby to choke. But if you are busy feeding or bathing or changing your toddler and your baby wakes up crying, if you can hear he or she is alright, then leave your baby to cry for a minute, it won't hurt them, if anything it will mature their lungs. Finish up quickly with your toddler without rushing them, don't let them realize you are trying to hurry up the process, and then go and tend to your baby.

Your baby doesn't know any better, for them it will become normal to have to wait a moment for you to finish with their sibling, but it will set a good foundation. Your toddler on the other hand is used to coming first, when you suddenly start pushing them aside to put your baby first then that is when they are going to start looking for negative attention. Make sure your first child is always sorted out first.

You also need to include your first child, or previous children, if this is your third or fourth, in the arrival and upbringing of your new baby.

When I went into labour with my son, it was 8:30pm. My daughter was already asleep, and unlike my first labour where I didn't know what to expect, this time I knew full well when I was in labour. I phoned my mum, who drove half an hour, to be with my baby girl whilst she slept. My hubby and I went to have our little boy. When my son arrived just before 1am, I told the nurse I wanted my daughter to come and see him. I wanted her to be the first to see him, before any photos were taken or anyone else had the chance to meet him. The nurse advised me that children under 12 weren't allowed in the ward but because there were no other moms and babies at that time she would do me a favour.

My hubby rushed home to fetch my daughter and my mum whilst I bathed. When they arrived back, my mom respectfully waited to be called. My husband and daughter came in and my son was wheeled out. The expression on my daughter's face was priceless. I sat with her next to me and explained that this was her brother from in mommy's tummy, and how sorry I was to wake her. I told her the reason we woke her up to bring her out in the middle of the night, "Zoë, I want you to know that this little boy, your brother, will be your best friend, you are the most important person in his life, more important than mommy, daddy, grannies or grandpas. YOU are the most important person to him," I told her. She was so proud. This wasn't our baby, he was *her* baby. Even now she calls him, "my boy."

From the time I got home and to this day my daughter has loved my son as though he belongs to her. They have the most incredible bond I have ever seen between a brother and sister. They have such an unconditional love for one another and would never intentionally hurt one another. When my son had just learnt to walk, I caught my daughter one day sitting next to him on a pack of nappies, she put her arm around him, kissed him on the cheek and said, "Judah, I'm so glad you're my brother, I love you." My heart just melted. I am truly blessed and thankful to God for guiding me and teaching me how to raise my children with love and understanding.

As with your first, you need to discipline your second child. It's so easy to compare your first and second with the thinking of, my toddler is older and understands so needs more discipline. Your toddler definitely still needs discipline but your second should be disciplined as your first was. If you want your second to be as full of love, discipline and understanding as your first child, then you need to raise them in that respect.

It is easier to instill good behavior and discipline from the beginning, than it is to unteach bad behavior.

Raise your second child to love their sibling, they also go through the "not wanting to share" phase, but this time there is constantly someone around who has a toy your baby wants purely because their sibling has it. In the beginning, I taught my daughter to distract my son with something else when he took her toy away. He was too young to understand that he couldn't have everything she had, so she would pretend something else was incredible and in turn he would drop what she originally had and take the next thing. Some might disagree with this but it allowed my daughter to play with what she had and there was no fighting over toys.

As my son is getting older now, there are times when he wants what she has but now he understands what he is doing. He now needs to be taught that he cannot take things from his sister. It isn't easy, but you have to step in as a parent. It's not your toddlers duty to teach your baby to share. When your baby takes something away from your toddler and your toddler is crying, it's easy to say, please take something else to keep the peace, I know I've done it countless times, but that just teaches your baby they will always get their own way and that is in no way fair to your toddler.

It is really difficult because it means having to deal with a baby who doesn't understand their emotional state, but when they take something from your toddler, you need to step in, take it away and give it back to your older child. Your baby is going to scream and cry, pick them up, explain they cannot take things away from their sibling and show them something else to play with. Then ask your toddler to please give the toy to their baby sibling when they are done. This teaches them to wait their turn and to share.

Raise all your children with good morals and a good foundation of Christ. Teach them to walk as Christ walked. To love their neighbor as themselves and not do to someone else what they wouldn't like done to them. Teach them good manners, please and thank you, not to be rude or arrogant, not to be bossy or think they are perfect. Teach them that they will make mistakes in life but you love them anyway. Teach them that their actions have consequences and they should always think before they speak or act. Teach your children what it means to let their light shine and that God loves each and every child regardless of what they look like, what their names are or what other people think of them. Teach them to be obedient. When my daughter doesn't listen I always say to her, when people look at you do you want them to think, "what a naughty child, look how she doesn't listen", or should they say, "wow, what a beautiful child, look at how she listens to her mom, look how she helps her brother and her mom".

On the rare occasion that my daughter does something hurtful, I explain to her that it hurts mommy's heart when she behaves that way, my daughter from a young age understood this and when a friend didn't want to hug her goodbye, she turned to me and said, mommy that makes my heart sore. It taught her the difference between what is right and wrong, what is hurtful and what is happy. It helps them to identify their emotions and gives them a foundation upon which their personalities form.

Decide now what kind of person you want your child to be and strive for that from the beginning. This is when they learn who they are, you can't one day realize you don't like who your children are and try to fix what you should've done in the beginning, it won't work. Raise your babies to be your legacy. Raise them into individuals you will be proud of, individuals people will be talking about long after you have passed from this earth because they made such an impact by purely just being themselves. God created them for a purpose, only you can teach them what that means!

The most priceless gift is Family

2016

CHAPTER 8

Cultivate your family

The most important job you have as a mom is making sure your family is always happy and healthy and that your home is running smoothly. You cannot raise your children the way God intended if your life is falling apart.

Your husband should always come first, as a mom this is something we often struggle with. Its hardest when our children are small, but you should always make time for your husband, communication, praying together, eating together, sometimes taking a bath together are all important. The most important thing which most woman don't wish to discuss, is your intimate relationship with your husband.

Your husband is a man. Men are created with needs, they can't help it. There's no on off switch, it's just on! If your husband is not satisfied within his marriage, within time he will go looking for someone who appreciates him enough to satisfy what he needs. For some it gets difficult after having children, you are so exhausted it's the last thing you feel like doing, but God made a sacrifice for your eternal life, Jesus sacrificed his life. If you are to love like Christ loves then it is a sacrificial love, you will get to bed, you may even sleep better afterwards you never know, but your husband needs you just as much as your children, if not more. He needs emotional support for the days at work when he is being drilled by bosses, clients, phone calls and a heavy work load, when in reality he would rather be at home with his family.

He doesn't go to work daily because he has nothing better to do, he does it because he loves you, he loves his children, he loves his family, and if he didn't work you wouldn't have a home, a car, the full closet of clothes or room full of toys. He does it to feed and support YOU. He sacrifices his whole day to work for you; surely you can sacrifice some time for him? If your husband is happy then you've done most of the work.

Cultivate your family to live a God centered life, knowing that without God you would all have no hope, you might not even have each other, you wouldn't have all the things God has done for you.

Find a routine that works for you. Spend time together as a family, have movie days where you all cuddle under a blanket on a mattress on the floor, take a walk in the garden, my children's favourite is when we all try to squeeze into the bath together and blow soap bubbles from our hands. It's the small things in life that make an impact.

Teach your children to not bombard your husband as he walks through the door, they can run and greet him with a hug and kiss but then give him a chance to get in and let out that breath of air that you also sometimes need. Make him a cup of coffee when he gets home so the only thing he has to worry about is removing his work boots and sitting for a second. Give him a minute to forget about the day he's had.

Try to have dinner ready by the time he gets home after work, this isn't always possible but try. A hungry husband is a grumbly husband, making sure food is ready, so when the hunger happens you can feed the family, is a way of keeping your home happy and peaceful.

Keep your house clean. I know how difficult this is when you have a baby, I had 2 of them. For the better part of 3 years our house was constant chaos, toys everywhere, clothes all over the bathroom and bedroom floor, dishes in every room of the house, it was a disaster. This caused constant arguments and frustration because after both having a difficult day we then had to do hurdles over washing and wash dishes before we could make coffee which none of us felt like. I would get frustrated because my husband wasn't helping me clean the house, even after he had been working all day. He was frustrated that I hadn't cleaned the house when I had been home all day. I get it, being at home with babies before they can walk or communicate is really hard. They need you for everything, they can't do anything themselves.

You need to find a balance though, I am ashamed when I think of what my home used to look like but we also had far too many things. I have given away and sold so much that we didn't need or use, I was such a sentimental person, I held onto broken things purely because of the memory behind them. We need to constantly look at things with an honest eye, do we *really* need that, possessions are replaceable, if you might use it one day, then you don't need it, get rid of it. If you do one day need it, it may not work anyway and you will need a new one. Since I came to this realization my home is always clean and tidy, everything has a place, granted I have children so there are times in the day where there are toys all over but every day they get packed away and cleaned up. I hated living in chaos but because we had too much nothing had a place. I do spend a minimum of 3 hours a day cleaning as well now though. If ever I feel lazy or tired, I turn on an episode of hoarders buried alive, and then I don't need much more motivation, then I'm up and cleaning. I find even now if I skip cleaning for one day, our whole life is upside down. My children seem to not listen to me, I get frustrated with everything and we are all generally unhappy. When my house is clean and toys are packed away my whole family is happy and my children are more willing to listen.

It's frustrating, I know, to pack away toys when your child is sitting behind you unpacking them, but do it once a day. My hubby taught me a song his mom used to sing for them and it helps my children to tidy up with me, particularly my smallest one. It becomes a game. He sings and packs away and everything has a place. They need motivating, they want to play not tidy up, and no matter how many times I've asked, they will not pack away one toy before taking another, I've come to realize it's because in their mind, they are playing with *all* the toys, not just one a time. As they get older it will change, but you cannot expect your children to be adults, we cannot deprive them of their childhood because they cannot go back and redo it. Make the one they have incredible!

Eat healthy, keep your home clean and tidy, pray together, discipline and be disciplined, spend time together, communicate and love one another and you will cultivate a happy, healthy family.

Grow in every relationship

CHAPTER 9

Cultivate your friendships and relationships with extended family

Once you have children, it is really difficult to maintain friendships with those who are single or who do not have children themselves, unless they are friends you have had since your childhood who are willing to walk this new journey with you as well. There are some friends you may have, that you don't have to see for years but you know that if you ever pick up the phone or meet up for a coffee, you can chat as though you have never been apart, no awkwardness or why didn't you contact me, but a catch up after missing one another for so long. These friendships are precious, treasure them as they are far and few between.

The newer friendships with single or non-parent friends are more difficult to maintain, it is hard for some people to comprehend that your life is suddenly not about partying, and that you would rather be curled up at home with your baby, than tearing up the mall in a massive shopping spree. They don't understand when they invite you for drinks at that new cocktail bar that opened down the street, when you respond with, "Don't you rather want to have coffee at the park where there's a play area?" They can't help it, but they really don't get it.

Don't be upset if these friends drift a bit, continue to keep in touch with them, one day they too will have children and they will need you when all of their friends just don't get it. They will then understand, and they will appreciate you that much more for never just letting go of them.

Your friends who do have children may seem easier friendships to maintain but these are just as difficult, not because they don't get it, but because their lives are just as hectic as yours. They too are trying to get their homes in order and keep happy healthy families, and it is difficult to sometimes get it right where you both have a gap for that catch up coffee. I have days where I feel like such a bad friend because I haven't even messaged to say "how are you", never mind the fact that I haven't seen my friend in over a month. And that's just one of my friends. Our lives are so filled with nappies, feeding, making juice and breakfast, lunch and supper, doing laundry, changing the DVD for your toddler, trying to listen to your children, working on your pc, cleaning the house and finding time in between to maintain your friendships. I find since having my second baby, I barely have time for Facebook, unless it's for my business. There are millions of photos of my daughter, but since my son arrived there's not half as many of either of my children that I, myself have posted. My days are so hectic that I will occasionally start a message to someone, and then my child will call me and I'll put down my phone and forget all about the message I was going to type or respond to.

The only time I really get to breathe for things like that is when my kids go to bed after 8, and by then I know my friends probably feel just as exhausted as me and should then be spending time with their husbands, so I don't really want to disturb their evenings. So it's a vicious circle, but we need to make time for our friends. The true friends will understand that your life is chaotic, make a date with them a few days in advance so that you both can work your routines around it.

Social media platforms have made it easy to stay in contact. I found that within my busy hurried life I would generally only speak to my mom. I created a WhatsApp group with my family members, (well with my mom's side of the family anyway) my mom, gran, aunt and uncle and cousin, this has been such a blessing. I don't forget to message anyone anymore and no one is neglected because I get to share what's going on in my life with everyone at once, we all share how we are and share photos of our children or homes or whatever is happening at the time. My family group pings constantly during the day but I love it, I love being able to see what is going on and share with them my proud moments as a mom.

In the same way, WhatsApp and Facebook, in the old days it was MXIT, are all ways to stay in touch with our friends and family. We need to maintain our relationships with our friends and family. Make time for them, it is important for your children to build relationships with their extended family as well and for them to make new friends. The first introduction to friendship for most of your children will be meeting your friends' children. Social interaction is such a vital part in raising our babies to fit into society. Not to be the same as everyone else and follow the crowd but to be able to communicate, engage, share, deal with conflict and get along with others. Your children learn the appropriate social behavior by watching how you treat and respond to those around you. If you are very reserved, quiet and shy and don't talk to just anyone, chances are your child will be the same, particularly a daughter. If you are a social butterfly and the world is your friend, your child will learn to be friendly and easy to talk to.

We have raised our children to be friendly from the get go, they would wave and smile and say hello to everyone. They need to also learn boundaries though, they need to know who they can and can't talk to and what they should and shouldn't say. They learn this again, from watching you and you from your teaching. My daughter struggled with understanding she couldn't just talk to anyone and tell them anything she wanted. We had to teach her it is dangerous to tell people everything. You can greet people but that's where it stops. She then didn't know who she could talk to. To her everyone is her friend, she can't decide who is worthy of speaking to or not and because she saw us greet and interact with people even though we didn't know them, eg. Petrol attendants etc. she couldn't establish who were friends and who weren't. So we made a new rule, when we were in town if someone greeted her she was allowed to greet back. If they asked her something like her age or name or where she lived, she would look at us, if we nodded then she could answer, if we shook our heads she was to be quiet, smile and look away. I would gladly explain to the person that I am trying to teach her not to speak to strangers, if they asked why she responded in this manner. So this is why cultivating our friendships is so important, it shows our children what it means not only to have a friend, but to be a friend.

Keep in touch with your friends, help your friends, when their baby is sick and they are not coping, take them some dinner, offer to get medicines from the chemist, give them a lift when their car breaks down. Be a caring, loving friend. Treat your friends the way you would like them to treat you, regardless of whether they do or don't. It doesn't matter if you seem to want to be their friend more than they want to be yours, God loves everyone all the time regardless of if we are busy or tired or can't make our morning quiet time because our child is sick, he doesn't love us conditionally based on how much effort we put in, he loves us completely and unconditionally, so if we are to walk as Christ walked then surely we should do the same?

Your friendships shouldn't depend on what you can get out of the relationships. I find not many people today grasp the true meaning of being a friend, being able to confide in one another knowing that your friend isn't going to go and gossip to someone else. Being able to pick up the phone and say I need you and your friend will drop everything to be there when you need them, friendship doesn't mean what it used to, for so many people and it is so sad.

Regardless of what type of friend you have or how much effort they put in, how tiring it is to maintain the friendship, you be the true friend, you do it! Love them unconditionally regardless, because that's what Christ does for you!

The most important relationship
you will ever have is your
relationship with God

CHAPTER 10

Cultivate your walk with God

It is imperative to understand that the only way to the Father is through the Son, Jesus Christ. Without Jesus our whole worldly population has no hope. Jesus is the way, the truth and the life. No one can get to the Father except through Him. This means, unless you have a personal relationship with Jesus, you cannot get to the Father and you will not inherit the kingdom of heaven.

What does it mean to have a relationship with Jesus? It means to walk with Jesus, and to walk as Jesus walked. When you choose to become a Christian, a true Christ filled Christian, you die to yourself, you leave all of your sin behind you and repent and turn from sin to focus on God and lead a good and edifying life. It means that Jesus is the epicenter of your life. It means that you base all of your decisions on, "what would my Father in heaven think about this."

I think back to the time when the WWJD bangles were brought out, the intention was excellent, but with no explanation people didn't really grasp the severity of what they were wearing. WWJD – What Would Jesus Do? We should ask ourselves this question every second of every minute of every day.

That movie you're watching, could you picture Jesus sitting watching it happily with you? Would he agree with the movie? If not, should you be watching it, if Christ is in you and you are in Christ? Before you open your mouth to speak gossip about the poor girl down the road who had an abortion because she felt she had no other option, think to yourself, would Jesus speak poorly of another to spread the news of that young girl? Do you not think she feels ashamed enough? Do you not think maybe that she needs Jesus? She felt so hopeless and as though there was no other option than to terminate the precious gift God had given her. Should you really spread that word to your friend who will pass it on to her friend and so on, or should you pray for her? Take it a step further, find her and visit her and pray with her. Tell her about the incredible God you serve. That being in Christ and walking as Christ walked, although it is not easy, it will deliver you and give you eternal life in heaven with our Father.

When you get home from the grocer and you unpack your groceries and you check your receipt, you realize you made a mistake and short paid. What would Jesus do? Would he leave it, there's nothing you can do, you're home already, I'm sure they won't make her pay for it. Or do you go back and pay the short change, or send someone nearby to do it for you that you could pay back later?

When you're walking through the shop and you see a lost child or a child who has fallen down, do you carry on walking and hope they will find their parents, or do you go to that child and help them either to find their family or to get back up off the floor and wipe their tears? What would Jesus do?

Your children get into the sweet jar and sit quietly in a corner and eat *all* the sweets; when you find them do you scream and shout and send them for a hiding, or do you think, what would Jesus do?

In everything in life, the ultimate question which should be on our minds constantly is, "What would Jesus do?"

How do we live a Christ filled life? Turn from all the things in life that Jesus would not do. If ever you find yourself doing something that you couldn't picture Jesus sitting doing with you, stop what you're doing and walk away.

The Bible says, "Love the Lord your God with all your heart", and "love your neighbor as yourself." My husband pointed out to me the other night, within these two commands, the 10 commandments are fulfilled. If you love God with all your being you will keep the Sabbath holy, you will not hold any idols before God or allow anything to take preference in your life over God. If you love your neighbor as yourself you would never commit adultery or look upon another man with lust or commit murder etc. Those two commands sum up what our whole lives should be like. If we could do just that then we would live as Christ does.

Christ is in you, when the Father looks at you, He sees His son; Perfect and blameless, but the only way the Father can see that, is if you are *In Christ.* Not just proclaiming to be, but walking in Christ, speaking in Christ, thinking in Christ and loving like Christ.

Spend time in prayer; devote your life to God. It is not easy, Jesus said, deny yourself, pick up your cross and follow Him. Deny yourself! Sacrifice! Suffer! Everyone hates the scriptures on suffering in the Bible, so many say, "I don't believe God wants us to suffer. We are meant to enjoy life." Yes and no, yes we are meant to enjoy life, but in the correct context. We can enjoy life by going surfing or fishing or playing with our kids or going for that coffee with our friends. Suffering is to not enjoy the sinful pleasures of the world, to not watch that movie that blasphemes and swears every second word, to not thrive on violence and horror movies, to not spread depressing gossip about others around you or news that is not yours to share; To not skip church so that we can go to a braai; to put God first in everything. To suffer is to deny yourself, to sacrifice your own time, wants and pleasures where they would otherwise take priority over your purpose. What's your purpose again? To love, praise, glorify and worship God and teach others to do the same. To live a life that God intended you to. To save the nations by being like Christ, that when others look at you, they see Jesus without you even mentioning His name. That is how we are to lead the nations and how we are to raise our children; that is how we are to honour our marriage. That is how we are to live!

Cultivate your life, grow your life, be the Mom that God destined you to be, not the washed out, watered down mother who would rather fob her children off on someone else so that she can enjoy her life until she is ready for her children. Instead be a Christ filled mom that raises and nurtures her children into Christ filled individuals who will be the herd dog for all the lost sheep. Cultivate your family, your marriage, your children, your life so that you can live the life and be the person God created you to be! You deserve it, your family deserves it and God deserves it!

Thank you, Father, for the devoted mothers who you have chosen for their little blessings. I thank you God that you are cultivating a new generation, one that will walk with purpose and with courage; courage to fight off the enemy and to know where they stand in Christ. Thank you Lord that being in Christ we know that the enemy cannot touch us.

I thank you Father God that your spirit will fill this precious mom reading this book, I pray that the words are of you and not of me Lord, I pray a discerning spirit that she takes away what is necessary from these words. I pray that nothing I have written be misunderstood or misinterpreted and this Mom would know that my heart is to share your love with her. To share the love I have of you and the love for my family and children with her so that she can understand the true love of God. I thank you, Father, for the mom she is and I pray you unlock her full potential of fulfilling her purpose. We know we are all sinners but I pray that you guide us in constantly living for our purpose.

Thank you for guiding us and teaching us the correct way of molding and raising our precious children. I pray a blessing over this mom's life, her marriage, her children and their future. In Jesus name, Amen.

In this book, I have chosen not to always quote scripture word for word with the scripture reference. The reason for this is with the hopes that you will look for them in your Bible. God's word has the answer to every problem we face in life. The only reason we can't find it is because we don't look for it. Several different versions of the Bible have been used when quoting scripture as I have chosen the version which easily describes the scriptures.

I challenge you to read your Bible for at least half an hour every day. It's not necessary to start at the beginning and work your way from Genesis to Revelations, although that too would be fantastic, but open to where God leads you. The one way God speaks to us is through His word, how can he speak to you if you don't even pick up the book. If you truly want a relationship with your Father and creator, dedicate time to read His word and pray. Listen to that still, small voice when God speaks to you and heed his warnings and conviction by the Holy Spirit.

If you are going through something and need someone to speak to or someone to pray for you, I would love for you to contact me. Again, I have no qualification other than being a Mom and a daughter of the most, high God, but I would love to connect with you and pray for you.

Website: www.cultivateyourlifeasamom.co.za

E-mail: michellebritnor@cultivateyourlifeasamom.co.za

Facebook: www.facebook.com/pages/Michelle-Britnor